Don't *be* Bitter *be* Better

From Terminal to Terrific, a Mother's Raw Account of Her Son's Aggressive Cancer Battle

Jennifer Webster

First published by Ultimate World Publishing 2022
Copyright © 2022 Jennifer Webster

ISBN

Paperback: 978-1-922714-75-6
Ebook: 978-1-922714-76-3

Jennifer Webster has asserted her rights under the Copyright, Designs and Patents Act 1988 to be identified as the author of this work. The information in this book is based on the author's experiences and opinions. The publisher specifically disclaims responsibility for any adverse consequences which may result from use of the information contained herein. Permission to use information has been sought by the author. Any breaches will be rectified in further editions of the book.

All rights reserved. No part of this publication may be reproduced, stored in or introduced into a retrieval system, or transmitted in any form, or by any means (electronic, mechanical, photocopying, recording or otherwise) without the prior written permission of the author. Any person who does any unauthorised act in relation to this publication may be liable to criminal prosecution and civil claims for damages. Enquiries should be made through the publisher.

Cover design: Ultimate World Publishing
Layout and typesetting: Ultimate World Publishing
Editor: Victoria Pickens

Ultimate World Publishing
Diamond Creek,
Victoria Australia 3089
www.writeabook.com.au

Testimonial

No one ever expects when you're in the prime of your life to be thrown into years of uncertainty about whether you're going to live or die—to even think about it is surreal. No one expects to spend years in mental and physical torment, plagued by the uncertainty of what new challenge tomorrow will bring. But that is exactly what happened to Matthew Webster.

Despite the enormity of the challenges ahead and the multiple invasive surgeries he endured, the last thing you would hear from Matthew is any hint of self-pity. In Matthew's world, every day is filled with a purpose, a single purpose to make certain that every minute of every day is consumed with getting on with getting better, and getting on with being better.

This core approach to life isn't born out of fighting an illness, it is a fundamental dictate of who Matthew is and who he will always be. Matthew's journey to wellness epitomises his attitude to life and his determination to succeed not just in beating this cancer, but in every aspect of life. Matthew demonstrates a clear mindset that is governed by courage and a tenacious approach in dealing with every task that is mixed with a healthy dose of good humour and positive energy.

It is impossible not to be inspired by Matthew's story and instead be motivated by his approach to life.

To know Matthew's story is uplifting, and to know Matthew has been my privilege.

Mr Steven Hoy, Retired Company Director

Dedication

This story is dedicated to Matt, for without him there would be no wild, unimaginable story to tell...and what a story it is!

In all my years of clinical practice, I have never come across a more aggressive, unrelenting, destructive case of cancer, especially in someone who was in the prime of their life.

It took an enormous amount of sheer grit, determination, and willingness to look this beast in the eye and affirm that Matt would be the victor, not the disease. His ability to turn the dark into light, to see the funny side of things and to joke with all those around him, diminished the gloomy atmosphere that so often accompanies a serious diagnosis.

At no stage throughout this entire transformative experience did Matt ever complain. He would sometimes say, "I am not too bad, there are people out there much worse off than me."

In my eyes he is a champion. Not only has he risen above any negative mind chatter, but he has overcome debilitating physical limitations enabling him to enjoy swimming, bike riding, hiking, and tennis, and all with an 'I can do' attitude.

This story could have ended disastrously, but Matt took everything in his stride and trusted that for every problem there is an answer, and it would unfold eventually.

> *"Life is 10 percent what you make it,*
> *and 90 percent how you take it."*
> **Irving Berlin (1888-1989)**

Contents

Testimonial	iii
Dedication	v
Foreword: A note from Matthew	ix
Disclaimer	xiii
Introduction	1
Chapter 1: Out of the Pan	5
Chapter 2: Into the Fire	19
Chapter 3: Burn Baby Burn	33
Chapter 4: Signs and Consequences	43
Chapter 5: Slice and Dice	51
Chapter 6: One Door Closes	61
Chapter 7: Another Door Opens	69
Chapter 8: The Master Plan	77
Chapter 9: Bring It On!	89
Chapter 10: Dogged Determination	97
Chapter 11: Rebirth From the Ruins	105
Chapter 12: Hope Strength Resilience	115
Afterword	123
About the Author	127
Speaker Bio	129
Acknowledgments	131
Testimonials	133

Foreword

A note from Matthew

There have been many nights where my parents, younger brother Alex, and his wife Belle have been sitting around the table, dealing cards and the topic of my somewhat unpleasant and bewildering tale has been raised. Although, unpleasant to outsiders, the experiences are often raised in jest and light heartedness as a means to temper the frustrations of coming second to me again for the fifth hand in a row. One thing that maintained its stability through the whole series of events was my ability to win a hand of cards in the most outrageous turn of events. These outrageous events are not too dissimilar to the journey which we all were unwillingly taken on, and our banter would often turn into a more serious discussion as to how these events would translate well into a novel and education tool.

That journey I'm talking about is the story of my diagnosis, battle, and management of cancer. The journey itself has many highs and many lows. Often not undulating like the ocean but rather is closer to a match in a boxing ring. Where the blows keep coming and the strategy needs to change until you can find some breathing room to ensure you can stay in the fight. After all, cancer is a fight for survival and this story portrays the lengths and effort not only myself but more specifically what my family and loved ones endured when the odds were not in our favour.

Don't be Bitter be Better

Where I am lucky and forever thankful is for my support network and immediate family. One of the greatest supporters during my fight was and will always be my mother. She was there to see every blow and there to discuss every strategy. I would like to say there were many late nights where we stayed up to discuss the results and discuss the next step. However, that type of mental agility and perseverance was beyond what my body could handle. These late nights were often had between my parents where they would discuss the ins and outs, and, in the morning, I would be debriefed about the previous night's thoughts. These thoughts would then turn into action plans and how we could achieve them in the most efficient and expedited way.

I believe these strategy sessions played into my mums' strengths. She is a woman of not only great intelligence and foresight but compassion and resilience. She has a stout passion for aiding and assisting others, and wants those in her life, be it personal or work, to live the healthiest and happiest lives they can. Her strategy often involved assessing the capability and limitation of the Australian medical systems and matching that with her own knowledge and experience on how to support and bolster the immune system of the human body.

These strategies are reflected in the following portrayal of events and are described from her perspective. The details are emotional and emphatically depicted to accurately explain the position of everyone involved. This emotional story from a highly empathetic point of view describes the trials and tribulation of the greatest fears a parent can have. It explains the extent everyone was willing to endure, none more so than my mum who ensured all energy spent was directed towards beating the odds, on the path to success.

Foreword

It is not only my mother's desire but also my own that this story can be shared with those who are looking for the next step, the next strategy to take on the challenges that await us. If this story doesn't provide the answers, then maybe it can deliver the perspective and reassurance that there is a way.

Matthew Webster

Disclaimer

This book is not medical advice; and does not seek to give medical advice. The story in this book depicts the author's experience and recollection of events and aims to broaden the reader's knowledge on integrative cancer strategies. The effective treatment of one type of cancer may not work against another type of cancer. All treatment options should be individually prescribed and personalised by a professional.

The information contained here is not intended to substitute the advice and assistance by a doctor or other medical professionals.

Introduction

It is every mother's worst nightmare to receive a phone call that brings bad news about one of their children. Especially when that twenty-four-year-old son was residing on the other side of the world.

On the 14th of June 2014, I received a phone call whilst holidaying in Far North Queensland (FNQ) with David, my husband and Matt's father, that will forever stay etched in all our minds.

"Hey, Mum, I'm in the hospital and things are not looking good for me. It looks like I have a tumour on my spine."

Holy hell! was our thoughts at the time, and they were not wrong. Hell with all the fire and brimstone was what it was going to be.

The news shocked us both, as we had only farewelled him six months earlier as he set off to travel and start work overseas. He was fit, strong, and eagerly looking forward to a new adventure and challenge. We had no idea what was to transpire over the next few weeks, months, and years.

It was only a few days after this phone call that he landed back in Sydney and we headed straight to The Royal Prince Alfred Hospital (RPA), located at Camperdown in Sydney, Australia, where he was met by a team of neuroscientists, and scheduled for surgery a few days later.

Don't be Bitter be Better

His diagnosis was confirmed six weeks post-surgery owing to the rarity of the pathology sample resected during the spinal operation. It was six weeks too long. He had a rare cancer, Angiomatoid Fibrous Histiocytoma a form of Sarcoma. Unfortunately, this finding changed to a much more aggressive diagnosis within another eight weeks, it was metastatic, meaning it was on the move. We were dealing with something that only a few people world-wide had encountered, and of those the majority had not survived. There was no road map or treatment strategy for this type of cancer, we were flying blind. There was very little research available for AMFH, and the medical evidence suggested that it was not an aggressive tumour. There had only been one other reported case of AMFH in Australia involving a tumour in the patient's hand, which was successfully resolved with surgery and radiation treatment.

Matt was always up for a challenge or new adventure, but this was not the adventure any of us had in mind. The human spirit given the right medium is truly amazing. The grit, determination, and sheer willingness to push through when things seemed exceptionally bad, gives rise to the true character of the man. Matt is one of four boys and a twin, which ultimately set him up to be competitive, outgoing, pragmatic, and it engendered the determination to persevere.

His go-in-and-go-hard attitude saw him through nine surgeries, six of them being major, plus six rounds of chemotherapy and thirty two rounds of radiotherapy, all within the first eleven months following the initial diagnosis and that fateful phone call that set this catastrophe in motion.

As we navigated our way through the myriad of specialists, surgeons, radiographers, and hospitals, I was grateful that we had sound medical knowledge and a good understanding of anatomy

Introduction

and physiology to fall back on. In our family we have five scientists including Matt. David is a Research Scientist, who searched endlessly for new treatment options, and I am a Health Scientist, Naturopath, Kinesiologist, Nutritionist, and also a Yoga Instructor. Alex is an Exercise Scientist, and Simon is a Geologist.

What a unique and empowered place to be. There was only one direction to go, and this was for Matt to get through this in the best way possible using both medical science and all the tools I had up my sleeve, plus utilising the top researched options we could find. We were waging war on this insidious disease, and we were determined to win. I made a promise to Matt early on that we would get him through this. I was determined to use every skill I had to help him survive. I knew that combining Complimentary Therapies with the finest of Medical Science would give him the best possible outcome. I was also aware that by altering the psyche and actioning a person's drive towards a reward or goal could shift the focus away from negativity to positivity.

This true account is written from my perspective. There were many hats that needed to be worn and interchanged sometimes hourly. Going from being Matt's mother, to researcher, nutritionist, naturopath, financial planner, as well as being there to give support to the family.

The trials we faced as a family and the unsurmountable challenges that Matt faced was not unlike being sucked into a giant vacuum, and into the depths of despair. We were continuously trying to claw our way to the top, putting out the fire storms and reaching for new horizons and positive news.

Chapter 1

Out of the Pan

The sensory overload of the tropics, the smell of the saltwater, the palm trees blowing in the breeze, 28° every day, and surrounded by lush tropical rainforest and wildlife. It sounds like paradise, doesn't it? It was winter, so David and I escaped the cold of Sydney to take one week out of our schedule to enjoy some solitude and relaxation in Far North Queensland. We had come to that time in our lives where we felt unencumbered by family responsibilities. Our oldest son, Simon, his wife, Kayla, and their two children had moved to Queensland the previous year, Matt had moved to South America six months earlier, and Michael, Matt's twin, had moved to Japan one year prior. Alex our youngest son was settled and doing well in Sydney.

Isn't this what every parent aspires toward? All their children settled, safe and doing well, and for the parents to be able to relax, travel and to have their own space and time. Colloquially known as *the golden years*. Even though it was a short break, we enjoyed six days of total relaxation in Queensland and were feeling refreshed and recharged, and ready to head back to Sydney and back to the grind.

We had arranged to visit Matt in Santiago, Chile in two and a half months' time. This would make it eight months since he left Sydney and it would be time to pay him a visit. We had been planning this trip for months and we were very much looking forward to it. We were keen to see where Matt lived and worked, and to get a feel for the place. From what Matt had told us, the people were lovely, and the scenery was spectacular. The three of us had planned to visit Easter Island for a few days, travel to Machu Picchu and then stay in Santiago. We had our accommodation and flights booked and were waiting with eager anticipation to see Matt again.

We were fortunate enough to have already visited Michael in Japan earlier in the year, and it was a great experience, but with our family split and living half a world away in opposite directions, we had already discussed that for Christmas we would meet at a central location. We decided that Waikiki in Hawaii was nearly equal distance from Tokyo, Santiago, and Sydney. We had planned to spend Christmas lunch with our extended family in Sydney and then to meet the boys on Christmas Day, in Hawaii. Two Christmas days back-to-back, Santa would be busy.

Then, on our final day in paradise, we received a phone call from Matt that would stay forever etched in our minds. It was the phone call from hell, the phone call you never want to get as a parent. I was initially excited that he rang, although I had been wondering why I hadn't heard from him for the previous six days whilst we had been away. It was highly unusual, and I had a gut feeling at that stage that something was amiss. At the time I thought he may not have wanted to disturb us on a holiday, but it turned out the perfect storm was brewing, and this phone call was its introduction.

Out of the Pan

"Life moves very fast. It rushes from heaven to hell in a matter of seconds."
Paulo Coelho - Brazilian novelist

As we answered the call, I was initially excited to be hearing from Matt, but this soon turned to a high level of concern as he reiterated the last twenty-four hours to us with a shaky tone to his voice.

"Hey, Mum, I'm at the hospital in Santiago and things are not looking good for me." I immediately had a feeling of dread, drop to my stomach. Matt is usually upbeat and excited when chatting about his adventures. I knew this news was not going to be good. As both David and I listened intently he went on to say,

"The pain in my back gradually got worse during the trip until it was unbearable. I've had extreme back pain, and weakness in my legs. I had to wait until I came back to Santiago to get medical help, as this is the best hospital in South America. I went into the office today, and I walked to the hospital from work, and they are running some more tests. I've seen three specialists and it seems I've got a tumour in my spine."

Was I hearing this right?

"You've got *what*, a tumour in the spine, are they sure?" The unthinkable happened, my God, I wondered how long it had been there.

A million thoughts were running through both mine and David's minds. Does he need urgent surgery, how big is this tumour, are they going to operate, does one of us need to jump on a plane immediately and go to the hospital, will this affect his walking?

We had so many questions running around in our heads but no answers yet.

Matt went on to say, "The doctors here have told me that treatment is needed urgently as the tumour has already caused partial paralysis and it appears aggressive. They will operate within three days if I stay, and plan to remove the tumour and implant titanium rods up either side of my spine. They have also spoken about radiation therapy as well, but they strongly suggest I immediately fly back to Australia for treatment. I need you to book me on the first flight out. I need to come home asap"

Can you imagine how you would feel if you received this phone call? Your son or daughter living half a world away dealing with this by themselves. I felt momentarily gutted, like the rug had been ripped out from underneath me. It was hard to fathom that my healthy, cheerful son had been in extreme pain for at least the last few weeks, and he now had a tumour in his spine creating havoc. It was difficult news to hear and digest when we were living so far away and could not be by his side to offer support at that moment in time.

That phone call immediately sent us into a spin. We were shocked and unprepared. A tumour in my fit and strong twenty-four-year-old son seemed unthinkable. How could this be? We had no further details, all we knew was that he had to pack up his life by himself and return on the first plane back. I was wondering how much he had been told, how he was dealing with it emotionally and what other details had he not disclosed over the short phone call. Our tropical utopia had just been shattered, but our thoughts instantly turned to promptly getting Matt home and into a hospital in Sydney. Our first stop was at the local airport to book him on the next flight back home. At the time I had contemplated whether I should fly to Santiago to be with him, because as a mum this was tough. I felt very strongly that he should not be there alone dealing with this news. I wanted to be there for him to offer support, encouragement, love, and to help him pack his belongings. At this stage it had been six months since Matt had moved to Santiago and six months since we had last seen him. As Matt can tend to play down personal problems, we had only been given a small glimpse of what had transpired over the last few weeks.

The doctors at Santiago Hospital had supplied Matt with a disc of his scans, blood results, a diagnostic report, a medical referral, and discharge all within twenty-four hours. He walked back to work to inform his boss and his work colleagues of the confronting news.

I can only imagine how Matt was feeling at that moment. He would surely have been in shock never imagining that what first presented as a sore back could lead to this. His work colleagues immediately swung into action and booked him a business class airline ticket and promised to pack up the rest of his apartment if needed. They were amazing. Matt only had a few hours to pack what possessions he could fit into a suitcase, thinking that he would return to work in perhaps a month or two. Within forty-eight hours he had been to the hospital, examined by three specialists, scanned, diagnosed, discharged, belongings packed, and on the plane back home. Matt arrived in Sydney the day after we arrived back from Queensland.

Don't be Bitter be Better

Behind the scenes

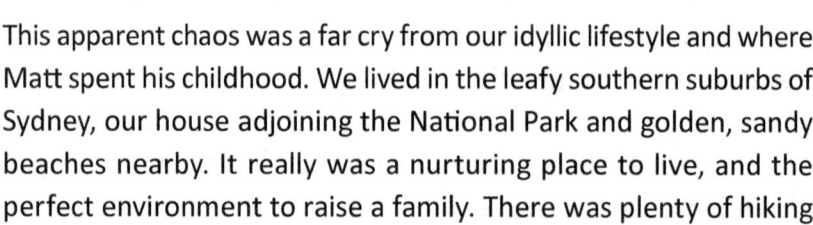

This apparent chaos was a far cry from our idyllic lifestyle and where Matt spent his childhood. We lived in the leafy southern suburbs of Sydney, our house adjoining the National Park and golden, sandy beaches nearby. It really was a nurturing place to live, and the perfect environment to raise a family. There was plenty of hiking in the bush, days spent at the beach, and being at one with nature when the kids were younger.

David and the boys

Matt is the second oldest of four boys and he is a fraternal twin to Michael, better known as Mick to the family. Simon is the oldest son, and Alex is the youngest. All the boys have a strong brotherly bond and get along well together. Matt's nature has always come across as being calm and confident, although he was adventurous as a child. If he was intrigued by something he fancied, he would just take off. When he was three years old, he took off from a children's playground, zig zagging his way across the street, dodging cars, running in and out of shops to satisfy his inquisitive nature. I'd never known a three-year-old to run so fast and disappear out of sight so quickly. I needed the assistance of the police to find him. He loves trying new things and has never been one to shy away from a challenge, which today still holds true. He has always been fit, played tennis, soccer, baseball, water polo and he was an excellent swimmer. As his teenage years progressed, he liked to run, bushwalk, go to the gym and was a volunteer surf lifesaver. He was also a member of the local high school band and had a great social network. He has a fondness for travelling, seeking adventure, knowledge and excitement. We had taken the boys on many escapades when they were young to spark their interest in nature, travel, and diverse cultures, allowing them to form their own opinions on world affairs.

Once he graduated high school, he studied Engineering (Materials) at Wollongong University being awarded an Honours recognition. This led to Matt securing a position as an engineer in a foundry in regional New South Wales (NSW). He leased a modern house and found some great housemates to fill the empty rooms. Many great times were had in this house complete with its own table-tennis table in the loungeroom. At one stage Mick moved in with them, as he had secured work nearby. It was an ideal arrangement for all the housemates. Matt thrived in his role at work, gathered industry knowledge and after twenty months was offered an engineer position within his employers South American office. He had a few months to increase his job specific skills and be ready for the role, and it also meant he had to move to head office to undergo further training. A mutual decision was reached between he and his girlfriend that he would do this for his career, whilst she finished her studies locally. This was a challenging and emotional decision for them to part, however they remained good friends and kept in close contact.

After a few farewell parties, on the 30th of December 2013, Matt boarded a flight for Santiago. Upon arrival he was met by a work colleague who assisted by storing Matt's two big suitcases whilst he set off for two months travelling prior to starting work. We would receive regular updates and we very much enjoyed listening to him regale in his adventures. During that time, he travelled to Argentina, Patagonia, Bolivia, Uruguay, Brazil, and Paraguay. He lived with a family in Bolivia for one week, he trekked volcanoes, learnt Spanish, swam in glacial lakes, visited The Witches' Market in La Paz, and rode a bike down Death Road in Bolivia. Death Road is known as one of world's most dangerous roads and also one of the most scenic. The altitude drops from 3,600m with sixty-four kilometres of winding road, going from snow-covered high altitude mountain ranges down to the steaming Amazonian Jungle. He visited the Potosi Silver Mine in Bolivia, which is not for the faint hearted or claustrophobics. One of the attractions is being able to hold a live stick of dynamite whilst having your photo taken, and praying the wick does not run out, and then promptly throwing it away as far as you can and watching it explode. Travelling by himself this offered Matt the opportunity to experience the adrenaline rush, the sense of excitement, the adventure, culture, freedom, and the chance to meet new people and experience change.

Death Road

During this trip he had decided to take a taxi from Argentina to Uruguay to cross the border. Upon reaching the border, the taxi was stopped, and it was soon surrounded by policeman bearing machine guns pointed at the taxi driver. The police were screaming in Spanish for Matt to get out of the car. They grabbed his luggage and told him to wait in the booth at the border. He was wondering what on earth was going on. He could understand some of the language, but as they were yelling and talking fast, he could not comprehend all of it. He was nervous in case they were going to arrest him as well. The taxi driver was arrested on the spot. It seems that Matt dodged the black-market butchers at the border crossing, as it was apparent that the taxi driver was taking Matt for organ harvesting. This was a close call and still makes my blood run cold. This near miss didn't deter Matt from continuing his trip, it added to the stories he could recount to friends and family.

Once Matt was back in Santiago, he needed to find accommodation. Unfortunately, he was unable to secure share accommodation, but he did manage to find a small flat in a nice area. His job description in Chile was regional engineer—his dream job. Matt has always been focused on a career path and what direction he would take in life. His strengths lay in his abilities to recognise and solve problems, mathematics, chemistry, identifying patterns, good people skills, and having a phenomenal memory. A career as an Engineer has played to his strengths, as he is a firm believer there is an answer for every problem. A true Engineer. Matt loves to travel, and with this job came a large amount of it. He was in his element and travelled to some beautiful locations. He engaged with many wonderful, kind people and was learning a lot about each country, workplace environments and how they operated. This job certainly ticked all his boxes. It was exciting, adventurous, challenging and there was never a dull moment.

While South America generally is magnificent, it does unfortunately have dangerous precincts where you must keep your wits about you. During his stay, he encountered both natural and personal threats, not previously experienced in his Australian upbringing.

Chile was encountering earthquakes almost daily, some resulting in tsunami warnings. On one occasion he and a work colleague were forced to evacuate from a seaside hotel and retreat to the nearby mountains where they spent the night in their work vehicle. Whilst not having encountered physical violence or threats in Australia he was subjected to a break and enter resulting in the loss of his work laptop, which was never recovered, but this pales in significance compared to witnessing a violent robbery in Brazil where a person was gunned down over the theft of a watch.

He had told us prior to going on a six-week work trip he had been experiencing severe pain in his back and was having problems sleeping. We thought it could have been the result of an unsupportive or old mattress, or that he may have torn a muscle or slipped a disc, and we hoped it would settle down. He did not want to cancel the work trip as he had a lot of meetings scheduled and he was already committed and looking forward to it.

Towards the end of that trip, he was on Copacabana Beach in Brazil enjoying the view and the culture. It was at this point that he knew his body wasn't quite right. He had put his right foot in the water and thought *that feels all right I wonder why there's not many people in swimming*. Then he put his left foot in the water, and it was freezing. He realised he had no temperature sensation in the right foot at all, and with his left leg he had noticed that he had minimal stability. He then and there realised this couldn't be good and he had serious misgivings about any delay in seeking medical diagnosis. He opted to wait as he was only a few days away from returning to Santiago where the second largest hospital in South America was situated. He crossed his fingers and hoped his body would behave until this anomaly could be explained. Within hours of him attending triage at the hospital, a team of specialists identified a tumour in his spine that was already causing partial paralysis. This was the first of many diagnoses and it signalled the start of his medical journey. Not only did it signal the start of his medical journey it also heralded the arrival of Team Matt, which consisted of family, friends, and colleagues.

I know for certain the family ethos is to embrace challenges. We love to play cards, board games, pool and when the boys were younger their competitive nature would come out when they played Monopoly. I feel this competitiveness and a love of challenges has played well into Matt's hand. We also don't like to be beaten by a challenge, the word loser is not in our vocabulary, especially when it involves the health of a family member. We had no idea how this story would transpire, we had hoped it may have been a simple fix and he could resume his life in South America, but that was not to be. There were so many hurdles and challenges along the way that sometimes it seemed insurmountable. It felt as though the universe was throwing everything at us to make life extremely difficult and challenging.

> *"When written in Chinese the word 'crisis' is composed of two characters. One represents danger and the other opportunity."*
> **John F Kennedy**

I was grateful that we had just taken one week off work. We were energised and ready to give Matt all the support he needed to get through the best way possible. Whether this would be emotional, physical, spiritual, or financial, we would make it work. This was a unique challenge, and I was in a unique position to help him recover.

Out of the Pan

There were many scenarios running around in my head at the time. What had caused this? Was it stress, was it an intestinal microbial infestation, was it diet related? What I did know was that a cancer diagnosis in anyone under thirty has a genetic component. Whilst I am Matt's mum, I am also a natural medicine practitioner specialising in herbal medicine, nutrition, naturopathy, cancer care and mind body wellness. My husband David is also a clinical nutritionist, researching diets and behaviour implications. Alex is a Strength and Conditioning coach with an Exercise Science degree, and his partner Belle is a Physiotherapist. Combining this with Matt being a resourceful engineer, I was sure we were well equipped to tackle Matt's predicament. After all I had been seeing clients who had challenging diagnosis in clinic and had managed to give many a positive outcome. It was game on.

Have you considered what you would do if you were faced with a situation?

Chapter 2

Into the Fire

As Matt's plane arrived early into Sydney airport, collectively we breathed a huge sigh of relief and couldn't wait to see him. I remember thinking, thank God he was now safely back on Australian soil, and he could pursue the urgent medical attention he required. David collected Matt from the airport and drove straight to the Royal Prince Alfred Hospital's (RPA) emergency department. We had undertaken extensive inquiries prior to his arrival to ascertain which hospital would be the best fit for his condition.

I arrived at the hospital after I had finished clinic that morning and was pleasantly surprised to see Matt looking quite well, albeit somewhat stressed. Stress would not be a word we had ever associated with Matt, he always seemed calm and in control, never letting things get to him. The hospital had already been forewarned of his impending arrival. With a medical imaging CD in hand, and the medical reports produced by the hospital in Santiago, he entered the world of emergency and specialist medicine. There were more scans to be undertaken, further blood tests, ongoing questions and a head to toe review. The team of specialists took a further three days before deciding on a plan of action, and it took another two days before the surgery was finally scheduled.

We found this process frustratingly slow, especially considering that the Head of Neurosurgery in Santiago had advised that he needed to have surgery within three days. The three days had already elapsed, and we wondered if his nervous system had been further impacted by this invasive tumour. During the review process Matt was not allowed to leave the hospital because of the uncertainty of the potential implications and unknown repercussions. The medical staff were concerned that if he moved around too much it may compromise the spine further and create additional pain, numbness, and paraplegia. There was a lot of sitting around in the hospital waiting for answers, results, and a surgery date, and it really tested our patience. Due to the complexity of the case the Head of Neurosurgery was assigned to his case. We were elated, as he had an excellent reputation and Matt would have a surgeon with years of experience. We felt that Matt would be in safe hands, although alarmingly there had not been any referral to an Oncologist and we were informed that this was not necessary until the tumour had been identified. I had an uneasy feeling about this and it did not sit well with me.

> *"Only those who will risk going too far can possibly find out how far one can go."*
> **T.S. Eliot (1888-1965) - Poet and Critic**

Finally, the day of surgery arrived. We were concerned knowing that part of Matt's spine had to be deconstructed to allow the surgeon to access the column of nerves that was the spinal cord. The surgery took hours, and during that time we felt quite anxious and tried to busy ourselves so the time would not drag on. All surgery has its risks, but as Matt was already experiencing partial paralysis and we knew the tumour had invaded his spine, it could go either way. We hoped that he would regain full sensation and the use of his legs without any complications. On the drive to the hospital the surgeon rang to advise that the surgery had gone well, however because of the intricate nature of the procedure he could not obtain clear margins around the tumour. This potentially allowed for some cancerous tissue to remain uncollected at the tumour site, with a further complication being that the sack encasing the tumour broke when he tried to remove it. To put this into perspective imagine having a small balloon filled with water and trying to squeeze it through a tight junction, then the balloon splits and the water goes everywhere. This is what happened at the surgery site in Matt's back, thus allowing the fluid containing cancer cells to enter the open wound and flow into the tissues and enter his blood stream. The surgeon then concluded that in his opinion the tissue looked malignant.

This was my worst nightmare!

I had hoped the tumour was benign and it could be completely removed without any further complications. Unfortunately, the sack broke inadvertently releasing up to two-billion malignant cancer cells into his body's circulation. I felt incredibly shaken, like I had been kicked in the guts. My immediate thoughts were how the hell is his body going to cope with this? I felt an immense pressure with the escalation of the intensity and urgency of the ensuing trauma. What was the next step in the medical process, if any, and how on earth would the medical team or I be able to eradicate all those cells using all my expertise in botanical medicine and mind-body awareness? *Holy Hell*, I thought. I needed to use all my skills as a complementary medicine practitioner to help get him through this challenge. I knew this was going to be one tough assignment.

Following the surgery, Matt was in hospital for another week. He had a steady stream of friends visiting each day, and the room was always full of laughter and mischief, which was great and took everyone's mind off the problem at hand, however one friend, Chris, was going through his own tough time.

Matt had known Chris since Kindergarten, and he was one of his dearest friends. His father had been diagnosed with a malignant brain tumour, Glioblastoma, only two months after Matt had left Australia. This was devastating news and upset Matt very much. During his primary and high school days Matt had spent many weekends at Chris's house with his lovely family being presided over by the dad, who was an imposing figure but a true gentle giant. Matt felt terrible that he could not be there for his friend, to support him whilst he was going through a very rough patch. This was tough for them both.

The pathology took three weeks and three professors to identify and diagnose. At a follow-up appointment with the surgeon, we were told that Matt had a rare tumour. The diagnosis was Angiomatoid Fibrous Histiocytoma (AFH). My anagram for it is AMFH, which stands for: a major fricking headache, and it would prove to be exactly that. We were advised that radiation would not be necessary as this type of rare tumour did not often spread, based on a handful of reported case studies worldwide, although my gut instinct was telling me that the cells had already escaped and this was not the end of it. The warning bells had been set off by the facts that the whole tumour could not be removed and the case enclosing it had split during the surgery. There appeared to be very little information or research about this disease because it was so rare, and there had only been one other case in Australia, therefore there were no treatment protocols. The news from the surgeon sounded promising, and we were more than surprised that no follow treatment was recommended. We were also excited that he did not require titanium rods up each side of his spine, as they can be restrictive with movement, and also that no radiation was recommended as per the advice of the Santiago medical team. The surgery was deemed successful, and Matt had regained both temperature sensation and stability in his legs.

We had hoped for a less invasive approach, as we were not keen on radiation or chemotherapy as both are very toxic to the body. The thought of our son being poisoned did not sit well. We were advised that only surgery was required, even though it was a malignant tumour it was considered low-grade. This was great news, the three of us were over the moon and felt relieved. Matt had been prepared for a more invasive approach, including surgery, titanium rods and radiation and we all thought this would be at least a three-to-six-month recovery. The surgeon also discussed that if Matt recovered well, he would be able to go back to South America to work. It was suggested that he could attend the Santiago Hospital for check-ups and the surgeon would be in contact with them. This sounded promising, and Matt was excited that he would be able to return to South America and continue his career path.

Less than two weeks after that appointment Matt started to get all the same symptoms back again, the weakness through the legs, back pain, and loss of temperature sensation. We tried to ring the surgeon and left messages, but these were not answered. Matt presented to RPA's emergency department, where the registrar ordered more scans and contacted the surgeon. We were then given the news that there was a mass growing at the tumour site. We had a sinking feeling in our bellies as we knew that this meant the tumour was more aggressive than we first thought. This time Matt did not have to wait long for the surgery. Less than two days later he underwent the second operation, and we were advised that three blood clots were removed from the original surgery site. We initially breathed a sigh of relief as we assumed it was positive news that it was just blood clots, but we were soon advised that this was the polar opposite, and the tumour was *extremely* aggressive. At this point I was annoyed, disappointed and upset for Matt and for his future. As we sat by Matt's bed in intensive care and the surgical team arrived, I asked why Matt's phone calls had not been answered. He had rung numerous times saying about the level of pain he was experiencing, of which could have been circumvented by a faster response. An apology was forthcoming, but the damage was done, and to add to our frustrations, an oncologist had still not yet been assigned to his case.

As Matt was recovering well from the second surgery, we requested a leave pass to visit the bistro across the road for dinner as it was only a short distance away. He had been unable to leave the hospital for the previous four days and he was keen to get out and get a bit of fresh air. He appeared to be walking well, but cautiously. As we sat down at the bistro, and we ordered our meals, we felt as though there was some normality creeping back into our lives. Once the meals were delivered and we started to eat, Matt felt a trickle down his back, and on closer inspection we saw that the surgery site was haemorrhaging. We were aghast with disbelief that this was happening! *What the hell was going on now?* Grabbing serviettes from the tables and applying pressure, we quickly made our way back to the hospital. The stabbing pain that had been there prior to surgery had also returned. The night staff contacted the surgeon, who advised that he would see Matt tomorrow. We left the hospital that evening feeling apprehensive and not knowing what tomorrow would hold. The stress levels were peaking in all of us, and our frustration was increasing dramatically. This series of events was not anticipated. The question on everyone's lips, where was this headed?

Into the Fire

I was now wondering whether he would have been better to undergo the surgery in Santiago and follow their suggestions even though it would have meant that one of us would have to move over there to be with him. We did consider this at the time when we received the initial phone call, however it would have meant that either I would have been absent from the clinic for three months or David would have had to go. The language barrier would have challenged us, and Matt would have been away from his friends and family during a very trying time. The pondering was quickly replaced with our considered opinion that our medical system was the best option at this point of time.

The next day when we arrived at the hospital, Matt was curled up in a foetal position in extreme pain. He looked shocking, and it was disturbing and distressing to see him like this. He has an incredibly high pain threshold, and always has, so we knew this was life threatening. The medical staff had given him painkillers to alleviate the intensity, but we soon learnt Matt was opiate resistant, which meant the strong pain medication had no effect. The wound site was haemorrhaging internally, creating a cascading waterfall of malignant cells flowing through his body. Our much loved son was now in a world of trouble.

After learning that Matt had a rare disease, we initially thought this was favourable news, believing there would be more interest in his case. The more doctors interested and investigating this disease should mean there was a higher chance of finding a targeted treatment. We couldn't have been more mistaken! The surgeon had little idea what he was dealing with, as how could he? There had been only *one* previous case in Australia, and it had not behaved like this.

Don't be Bitter be Better

As Matt lay there in the foetal position in excruciating pain our frustrations grew even further. The surgeon did not want to operate again, as three spinal surgeries so close together was unheard of and somewhat dangerous. Our view was, it could not be any more dangerous than what was already happening. He needed that surgery now! The surgical team decided to wait and see if the bleeding would stop by itself, but it didn't. Ten days after the second surgery he had a third surgery where larger margins were excised and then cauterised. Now his weakened body had succumbed to a total of ten days of malignant cells travelling through his bloodstream and into organs. This was devastating and turning into one huge nightmare.

I had been working in clinic during the day whilst David was at the hospital with Matt. Each day we would take him a home cooked meal and a fresh vegetable juice, as the preprepared foods that were being served were not up to the standard I felt were required to heal and adequately nourish a convalescing patient. I would go in after work and spend between three and four hours with Matt, talking over the events from the day or playing cards. During the time of the third surgery Alex woke one day feeling very unwell. He knocked on my clinic door, looking pasty and overall sick, with abdominal pain and I was pretty sure he had an appendicitis. The logistics of having the two boys in different hospitals was not plausible, so I drove him to RPA Emergency where my suspicions were confirmed. He underwent surgery the following day which was successful, however, he had an adverse reaction to both the morphine and antibiotics that were prescribed. Talk about out of the pan and into the fire. Coping with Alex being so ill and motionless from the medications, and Matt being one floor up having had three surgeries in such a short period of time, tested our mental and physical resilience.

Thank goodness for Alex's partner (now wife), Belle, who was there for all of us, but especially for Alex. She cooked meals for us, cleaned, and looked after Alex. Stress affects us all differently and I can only assume that the events of the last two months had adversely affected Alex's health too.

As Matt lay in the hospital bed recovering, a sprightly older gentleman in a grey suit entered the room and introduced himself as Martin. He had been contacted by the surgeon as he was the Professor of Oncology who looked after unusual cases or rare diagnoses. At the time we were playing cards with Matt, and Martin wanted to know what game we were playing.

Matt said, "We can deal you in, we're playing Asshole."

A wry smile crossed Martin's face as he chuckled then redirected the discussion. He explained to Matt that he would need radiation treatment and that he had already consulted the radiologist. Reflecting on the progression of the disease he remarked that the condition is difficult to contain once the horse has bolted, and the horse had well and truly bolted by this point of time! He stated that if he had been consulted earlier, he would have given Matt a light course of chemo tablets which may have prevented the bleeding. This added more stress, as we were now hearing differing opinions and advice regarding treatment as the individual specialists came to loggerheads.

The power of words

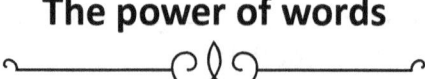

Matt's post-surgical review with the surgeon shattered our hopes of an early resolution to this calamity and our travel plans. As we sat there in his clinic, Matt was now being counselled that this tumour was extremely aggressive, and that he had a dark cloud hanging over his head and an uncertain future. Returning to South America was now out of the question. We told the surgeon that a family holiday to Hawaii had already been booked for Christmas time and we were very much looking forward to it.

He looked at Matt and said, "Yes, you need to go live your life and have fun."

We walked out of that office with three different attitudes. Matt looked upset, shocked, and deflated, like the wind had been taken out of his sails. David was more matter of fact, and although upset he looked at the facts and said, "It is what it is." I was dismayed on several levels. Matt had gone from 'surgery is all that is needed' to 'now go live your life and have fun' in the span of four weeks. What was he inferring? It seemed incredulous that in a matter of weeks our reality had been completely turned upside down.

This matter of fact-ness did not resonate with the way I would have presented that news in a clinical environment, especially for a younger person. Holistic practitioners tend to apply an empathetic and understanding approach towards the client, and consider the impact that this information will have on their overall wellbeing. I had decided early on that there would be no negativity and that we would just build on the positives, improve strength, provide support, and encourage resilience. As with any client, I personalised a health regime for Matt, using supplements, nutrition, botanicals, and homeopathy to improve his immune system and increase resilience. A positive mental attitude can go a long way to aiding a person's overall health which I am always fostering. We would get on top of this as we are a great team and together, our can-do attitude will prevail. We would be going to Hawaii, as I felt it was important for the boys to be together and to have fun.

> *"Every thought creates form on some level and all that our physical experience is – is a reflection of our thoughts."*
> **Marianne Williamson**

How high can you jump?

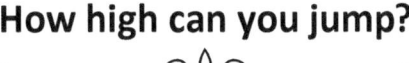

We were beginning to encounter many hurdles, although we were only three months into this experience. It felt like our world was crumbling down around us, and the challenges kept coming quick and fast. When I originally booked Matt's airfare back home, the company he worked for in South America also reserved him a business class fare on the same flight. As two different travel agents in two different countries were utilised, the local agent that I booked through took it upon themselves not to refund the flight. I was amazed that the two seats in the one name on the one plane were not flagged at the gate or on the booking system and the ensuing debacle could have been avoided. After months of going through different channels, we were told Matt could have a credit to go back to Santiago, but it had to be used in twelve months' time. This was unachievable. Eventually the agent reconsidered and issued him with a flight credit to the same value that could be used locally or internationally, although it still had an expiry date of twelve months.

The next hurdle was the health fund of which Matt had been a member of since birth. Before he left Australia, I had been advised by the funds' local branch manager that his policy could be kept on hold for two years, if overseas. Matt could resume it at any time within the two years. After returning home Matt went to reinstate it but they said the policy had changed, and he was no longer covered. The fund had changed their policy and the two year "on hold" no longer applied. I was exasperated as he had only been gone six months and we had not been notified of any changes. After much correspondence with the state manager his policy was reinstated with full benefits. Then there was Centrelink, they informed us that Matt was not sick enough to receive benefits, which was unimaginable. *Not sick enough!* Three spinal surgeries, radiation doses, and an aggressive malignant tumour, and he was not sick enough. This was another battle brought to a halt by me assuming control, I almost carried Matt to the Centrelink office so they could see for themselves just how unwell he was. Reluctantly, they conceded.

> *'Nil carborundum illegitimi' is Latin for 'Don't let the bastards grind you down.'*
> **General "Vinegar Joe" Stilwell**

No hurdle is insurmountable when broken into manageable chunks. This was our tactic, thinking through the problem, looking at the options and not accepting bureaucracy at face value, after all they are just people hiding behind a logo. We managed these challenges by taking one day at a time and always looking toward a brighter future. I hatched a plan, that our cancelled trip to South America (golden carrot) would take place once Matt was feeling strong enough. This allowed for a positive focus and purpose.

For over thirty years I have practised Yoga and drew heavily upon it for mental and physical enlightenment. This was the only opportunity I had to experience my happy place during these chaotic times. It was exasperating as a parent to see my son fading away and it took all the strength, I could muster to remain calm and not become disillusioned with the medical system.

I needed answers to some philosophical questions.

What was the universe trying to convey?

Who was the lesson for?

Was it for Matt, or all of us as a collective family?

Whatever the purpose, it was not yet apparent.

Healing Herbal Cream

90ml Jar

Combine equal parts
1) Emu Oil
2) 100% Aloe Vera
3) Base cream with 5 Bach Flower essences for shock

Add
- Essential oils 5 drops of each.
- German Chamomile
- Rose hip
- Everlasting

Mix together and keep in the fridge. Apply after radiation treatment and up to 3 x daily to reduce the likelihood and severity of burns.

Chapter 3

Burn Baby Burn

We were now forging a new path in uncharted territories, and I had some uncertainty of the road ahead. A specialist team had been appointed to Matt's case that we affectionately called, The Brains Trust. We felt as though we were between a rock and a hard place, that is between our holistic beliefs and accepting toxic oncology. This was Matt's health that was at question, damned if you do and damned if you don't. We understood that the radiation treatment would be necessary to cease any internal bleeds and mop up any nearby malignant cells. We struggled with the perceived conflict of doing-no-harm and delivering Matt to the Radiology Department, to be intentionally burnt as part of his treatment.

To maintain the holistic integrity, I made a soothing botanical cream to apply to the radiation site after each treatment which proved to be beneficial. This was to ensure that Matt would not suffer from radiation burns or end up with a weeping rash. I also prescribed immune modulating, hepatic support and adaptogen botanicals to aid in his overall well-being and to keep his energy levels optimised during treatment. These were targeted herbal medicines and nutraceuticals that I concocted specifically for Matt's constitution and disease state. After thirty rounds of radiotherapy, and five weeks of travelling daily to the city, in addition to three major surgeries Matt remained strong and focused mentally, even though his body was looking battle scarred and tired. Some days he chose to catch the train to the city and walk to the hospital, which was easily a three hour round trip. This gave him the opportunity for some much needed 'me time' away from us and he got in some exercise as well. Once the radiation treatment had ceased it was time for Matt to undergo another PET scan—a scan that checks for diseases in the body. We were quite hopeful that nothing sinister would appear on the scan.

Around this time, we needed to allocate family resources to assist Matt, although he was still doing everything himself and was independent, we knew he needed back-up. The weeks were consumed with doctor appointments, scans and treatment schedules that needed one of us to be there with him. The drive into the city would take an hour each way, and if he was having treatment, we could be in the city most of the day. It was important for us to be there and support him every step of the way. It became apparent that it was going to take a lot longer to get him through this than we had originally thought. We decided that David would be Matt's carer/driver/assistance/cook for however long it took. This meant I was now running both businesses by myself, and juggling being a mum, clinician, and Matt's holistic prescriber. It was an understatement to deny how hectic our lives had become.

> *"Adopting the right attitude can convert a*
> *negative stress into a positive one."*
> **Hans Selye (1907-1982)**

During October we started to organise our holiday to Hawaii. We were all very excited to be able to catch up with Mick, to relax, unwind, and have a fun Christmas together. Frustratingly only one month before we were due to fly out, Matt's PET scan revealed some tissue abnormality within the pancreas. The endoscopy summary was inconclusive as the doctor was unsure of the results, and because of this we wondered if perhaps the radiation may have damaged the pancreas. The doctors request to conduct a biopsy was denied by us for fear of spreading this disease even further. This decision was not made lightly, but it was definitely the right decision given the ferocity and rapid growth of the cancer cells.

The surgeon who conducted the endoscopy remarked that he had never seen anything like this within the pancreas. He said it was very odd, and he didn't know what to make of it. He suggested obtaining a second opinion. We had been hearing this admission of uncertainty a lot; "We have never seen this before, we know nothing about it, there is no protocol or treatment for it." These admissions were unsettling and unnerving and didn't do much for our confidence of the medical system. They were trying, but it was new territory for everyone involved. I felt we just needed to get on that plane to Hawaii, have fun, refocus and relax for ten days. That was my prescription to think, breathe and unwind.

We arrived in Hawaii on Christmas Day and celebrated that night in Waikiki. It was refreshing to be away from the hospital system, the doctors, pathology labs and the whole routine of the last five months. We had to reacquaint ourselves with feeling normal again. After a few days in Waikiki, Matt, Alex, and Mick flew to the Big Island of Hawaii to do some hiking and exploring, and to see the big volcano. They had an amazing time and lots of fun just being brothers reunited. They swam in an awesome rock pool with green sea turtles, saw the lava in the volcano and marvelled at the beautiful scenery. This was soul food for the three of them.

Don't be Bitter be Better

David and I managed to half relax for three days in Waikiki, but in the back of our minds we were wondering what was going on in Matt's body. When the boys returned, they looked refreshed, tanned, and relaxed, although Matt said he had pain and tightness in his hamstrings and glutes. We thought perhaps he may have overdone it as he was still recovering from radiation, but the pain did not seem to subside. One evening when we were playing cards and I was discussing resilience, being positive and getting through this, he said he was trying his hardest, but he felt that he could no longer trust his body. Imagine finding yourself in this predicament, sensing that your body is trying to kill you. This was a very disturbing revelation and gave us one of the few glimpses into his innermost thoughts.

Hawaii 2015 (Matt, Alex, Michael)

Happy New Year!

We celebrated New Year's Eve, 2015 on Waikiki Beach with a huge crowd and lots of fireworks. Cheering each other we wished for fantastic health, happiness, and good fortune for the year ahead. This was a happy distraction, one of the few that could momentarily transport us away from gravity of Matt's illness. On the surface he was coping but perhaps those words from the surgeon had stuck in his mind, or was it the body he couldn't trust giving him hints that it was up to no good again? All too soon our holiday was over, and once again we prepared ourselves to be back on the 'hampster wheel' of the hospital system.

Matt flew back to Sydney two days before us as he had an appointment with a hepatic surgeon to further investigate the previously seen shadowing on the pancreas. The surgeon placed the scans on the lightbox and immediately pointed out a tumour in his pancreas, confirming what the previous doctor had seen but had been unwilling to label. This was a huge shock to all of us. The surgeon said he needed to operate as soon as possible. As I was still in Hawaii, I rang the surgeon to inquire about the surgery and the tumour, and what this would mean for Matt and his ongoing health. He said if he was in the same predicament, he would have the surgery as there was no evidence of cancer anywhere else on the recent PET scan (proven later to be incorrect). My immediate thought was; *is this latest tumour due to the bleed and disbursement of the malignant cells from the spinal surgery?* I had queried his neurosurgeon some months earlier, concerning the location of the primary tumour in the spine and the relationship those nerves had with the pancreas. This fell on deaf ears as there was no understanding of Eastern Medicine philosophy by a Western Medicine doctor. We were shocked and upset that the cancer had metastasized to the pancreas, but I instinctively knew that there was a relationship to that area of the spine, and I could see the trajectory where this was heading.

A few days after we returned from Hawaii, Matt went in for surgery to have part of his pancreas resected and his spleen removed. Martin, the oncologist, was closely monitoring his case especially as there had now been another tumour site. Recovery from the surgery was slow with his digestion now compromised, and he experienced a sizeable drop in weight. There were no dietary instructions or nutritional advice from the hospital upon discharge, fortunately both David and I put together a moderated nutritional eating plan. One week post discharge we had to make a trip to emergency department as Matt was experiencing a severe discomfort near the surgical site. It seemed that after every surgery there were unwanted side effects. A gastroscopy was performed, and after another few days recovering, he was sent home feeling better.

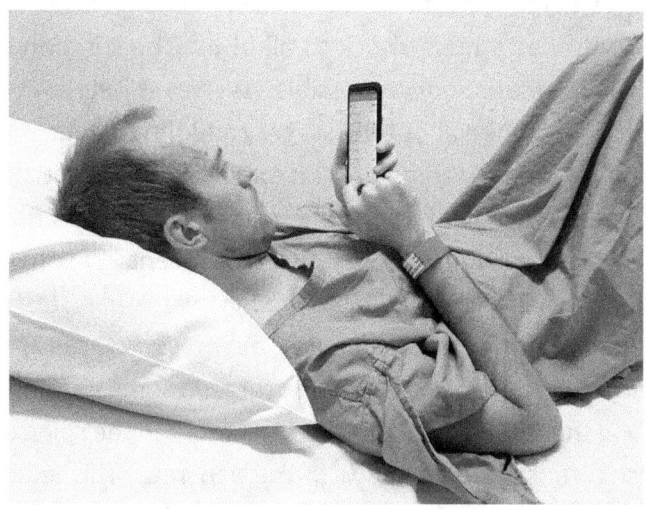

Matt in Hospital

Since this disease had now metastasized to the pancreas, I felt it was imperative to step up the integrative health program I had for Matt, thus requiring a GP to administer intravenous (IV) vitamin C to improve Matt's immune system and recovery. It is well documented and researched to be effective for acute or chronic illness. Locating a doctor to administer this can be difficult. I chose a well-known one, that was not too far away, who was also aware of my practice. I managed to secure an appointment quite quickly, however when we walked into his clinic and I explained the story so far, he turned to me and curtly said, "Well what do you expect me to do that you have not already done?" I can only presume that he knew of my work with oncology patients and questioned what he could offer that I could not.

This was not the response I had hoped for, I was aghast, taken aback. Matt looked incredibly sick, and I was doing all I could as a practitioner and mother to get him through, but I also wanted him to have the IV vitamin C as I was not legally licenced to administer it. This treatment was agreed to, but the environment was not as sterile as we had hoped. The room had many people in it, with different conditions, and we felt it was not a safe environment for someone whose immune system was severely compromised. We only went there a few times as Matt was concerned about the potential risk of infection from such a busy waiting room.

A few weeks later we were booked into see Martin as a follow-up. He was quite concerned upon seeing how emancipated and drawn Matt looked, and suggested we consider undertaking pathology testing from an overseas laboratory. With a look of concern on his face he told us we would have to spend some of our hard-earned cash to see if they could locate the best course of treatment for Matt's rare disease state. The lab was called Foundation One and was located in Cambridge, Massachusetts. They use comprehensive genomic profiling to search 324 genes for cancer relevant mutations in the DNA of the tumour, enabling the doctor to explore treatment options. We were excited about this, as so far it seemed the radiation and the surgeries had really done nothing to resolve the situation. The cost to have this analysed was $7000 USD and it would take six weeks for the pathology and treatment options to be returned to Martin. We were extremely hopeful of Foundation One finding a targeted treatment option for Matt. We already knew chemotherapy was not always successful in treating sarcomas let alone this rare variant. Whilst we were waiting for the results, the pain in Matt's glutes and hamstrings was becoming more intense and he was looking like death warmed up. It had now been three months since the last PET scan, so another one was ordered to check for disease progression.

> *"It is more important to know what sort of person has a disease than to know what sort of disease a person has."*
> **Hippocrates**

There were so many unanswered questions and possibly the biggest one was why this had happened to Matt. Realistically, the answer is *why not*, as it could happen to anyone at any given time. There are so many misconceptions about people who develop cancer. Speculation such as they made it happen through bad attitudes or negative thinking, or they have a bad diet, or they drink too much or they smoke, the list goes on. The truth is, cancer is multifaceted. All the above may or may not be contributable, but then there are other factors that come in too. Genetics, hormones, environmental toxins, and age can also be thrown into the equation. Take for instance young babies that are born with tumours, or children under ten years old who develop them, we can't accuse them of drinking or smoking or having a bad lifestyle. The truth is cancer does not discriminate and it can happen to any one of us at any time.

Stress can also be a major factor and can be one of the contributors to many disease states. We feel Matt had the perfect storm to form this disease. All the ducks lined up and *wham*! Perhaps not surprising as we have a family history of cancer. He was twenty-four when diagnosed and our research shows us that of the few cases worldwide most were males aged around twenty-four, which would suggest hormonal influence. The younger you are the more aggressive the cancer. Even though Matt never appeared to get stressed and he was excited about moving, I feel the build-up of relocating to another country, starting a new job, missing his girlfriend, finding new friends, and nearly losing his kidneys, may have contributed to tipping his body's defences over the edge. We will never know exactly why, but we do know it was multi-faceted, and it was not just one issue that caused it. Some might say it was fate or bad luck, but we believe it was the perfect storm. Curiously, some of his friends use to envy him and his ability to set and achieve ambitious goals. I feel this was from his happy-go-lucky nature and his positive attitude where he would strive for what he wanted, determined to succeed, and usually did. Quite often they would say to him things like 'I want your life,' however, I seriously doubt they would say that now after what he has had to endure.

There was a huge realisation that Matt's life had changed irreversibly due to the physical impact. Three surgeries on his spine which had weakened that area and now half his pancreas was missing, the spleen was gone, and our cherished son's life was on the chopping block. We remained steadfast and rational and aimed to steer this ship in the right direction, as we were not going to let it sink. I have always advocated whole body care and it was even now more imperative than ever. With each step along the way I ramped up the herbal medicine, the targeted gold standard immune modulating substance (Arabinoxylan) compound hydrolysed enzyme complex,

Don't be Bitter be Better

and wide range of supplements. As with every patient Matt's script was individualized taking in to account his current health status, the disease and severity, plus known contraindications from pharmaceutical drugs. We kept the fresh juices and healthy meals coming for Matt to keep up his strength and allowing his body to repair as quickly as possible. I felt like a fire warden running around like crazy putting out the spot fires because there was no way that I was prepared to let my son burn.

Chapter 4

Signs and Consequences

Being mindful and aware of my surroundings is a way of life I embrace as it enables me to stay grounded and calm. It is as though this is my internal compass, something that is either innate or learnt during my formative years, and these guiding principles are embodied in my daily life. I firmly believe that nature and our surroundings can always provide the answers if we are willing to be receptive, listen with intent, feel with our heart, remain aware and read the signs mother nature so often sends us. To ignore it, is to one's detriment. We noticed a myriad of strange occurrences from the beginning of this life changing event. When we received that fateful phone call from Matt in June, we were driving peacefully through a beautiful lush tropical landscape, and as I glanced up towards the sky, I noticed a dead bat dangling from the power lines. I immediately felt uneasy in the pit of my stomach. I tried to look away and ignore what I'd seen, but you can't unsee a sign. In ancient mythology bats represent a dark energy, and interestingly South America has also been known as the land of the dark souls. This set my alarm bells off and I wondered whether there was an association between the dark side and what may have taken hold of Matt. What did his predicament have to do with what I just saw and what was the implied message?

Don't be Bitter be Better

"Have courage for whatever comes."
Mother Teresa

A few days after arriving home from Far North Queensland we noticed multiple weird, red ugly plants appearing in our back lawn. These plants are called Devils Finger, also known as Devil's Dipstick, and is a rare fungus. This was extremely odd, as we had lived at the property for over thirty years and these fungi had never appeared before, nor since. It was a very unusual phenomenon and seemed to creep into the bat theme about darkness and negativity. The tumour in Matt's back was vascular, meaning pertaining to the blood and veins (AMFH) and these devils finger plants seemed symbolic of the growths that were appearing inside of Matt. Yet another sign we could not unsee. Prior to departing to Queensland our bedroom door had started to creak frequently, even though we had oiled the hinges. It had been incredibly annoying well before our departure and persisted beyond our return. I suspected that something was amiss when this commenced, but now realise it was a yet another sign and perhaps even an early communication of impending trouble on the horizon.

Devils Finger

Signs and Consequences

Near Matt's bedroom there is a passageway where native violets started to grow profusely through the grass. They are beautiful purple flowers with sunny faces, and they really brightened that area. Coincidentally, Sweet Violet is a traditional herbal medicine used to treat malignant disease and helps to protect against the spread of cancer. There is an understanding amongst herbal practitioners that plants with healing powers propagate in regions where they can be of most benefit. The violets were yet again another sign that in hindsight could have conveyed a need for greater awareness. I also started to notice that random white feathers would appear in odd places including my handbag, on my desk, on the path in front of me, and there were too many occurrences to be coincidental. Once I ordered a second-hand book online and when I opened it at a random page a small white feather appeared. I took this as a positive sign that Matt would be looked after.

After waiting weeks to hear back from Foundation One, Martin presented us with their findings that concluded, "We wish you luck, as we have never seen this before." The doctors had studied the pathology slides that had been flown over to the United States, and ran their database against the tumour material, but alas there were no matches. It appeared that this tissue sample may be some type of hybrid neoplasm (an unknown, unnamed cancer). This was also at a time when genomic testing was in its infancy. We were gobsmacked. The world's largest bank of pathologies and diseased states, and yet they came up with no matches. This was proving to be very difficult to treat especially when there was no research basis to work from.

It was a case of *strap yourself in as you are now going on a hell of a roller coaster ride*. Martin looked as deflated as we did. We knew the answer had to be out there somewhere and we kept looking. At this point Martin informed us that the disease was now metastatic and aggressive which meant, it would be difficult to control. It had already invaded the pancreas which was the first recorded case worldwide. There was also another disease site located in his left shoulder on the last PET scan and this was already creating a tonne of pain. We now knew it had the ability to quickly spread anywhere in the body, it was indiscriminate and had already attacked bones, muscles, and organs. We had secretly wished the Foundation One DNA testing would be the Holy Grail of answers, instead their zero findings hung us out to dry like the dead bats.

Matt needed radiation on the shoulder and Martin also recommended intense chemotherapy to commence as soon as possible. This had now gone from bad to unimaginable. It was hard enough to reconcile with the radiation treatment, but the thought of chemotherapy being injected into Matt was horrifying. Both the neurosurgeon and hepatic surgeon felt that chemo would not help his situation, however, Martin was one of Australia's leading experts in sarcoma treatments and rare and unusual diseases and he was at the coal face in Boston at the start of chemotherapy. His opinion was something that we respected and considering the rapid spread of the disease we were left with little to no options. At this stage I let Martin know my profession and I gave him a comprehensive list of everything that I had prescribed for Matt. We discussed it and I told him my reasoning for Matt taking a wide range of supportive adaptogens, herbal medicine, and a long list of supplements. He was supportive of our endeavours. I expressed that my intention was to keep Matt on an ongoing regime of personalised targeted therapies especially whilst he was on chemo as it was so toxic.

Signs and Consequences

Now, I needed to notify Mick in Japan about Matt's progress, it was a phone call I was dreading to make. Twins have an incredibly special relationship, as they have been together in utero, and in the formative years of their lives. They always have that special other person who understands them like no one else will. Just weeks before we had to fly Matt back from South America, Mick advised us that he was taken to the hospital as he was experiencing strong chest pains while at work. He was quite concerned, as were his workmates and the doctors, but after many tests it was ascertained that his heart was okay, and the pain was from a torn ligament. Interestingly the pain that Matt had in his back from the tumour was directly located behind the heart. Perhaps Mick was picking up Matt's pain from across the globe, and this was another shared experience.

Making that phone call to tell Mick that Matt was now in a world of trouble, and the cancer had spread was extremely difficult for me. When I told Mick the cancer had spread, he was shocked as he thought Matt just had a tumour, and it was now gone. This disease was threatening that incredible twin bond by compromising Matt and threatening his mortality. This was heartbreaking and difficult as a mum to relay this message over the phone. There have only been two times during this whole episode where I felt bereft and this was one of them, the other time was when we were told the tumour was malignant. It was a matter of gathering myself together, digging deep, staying determined, and standing alongside Matt to fight and win this war.

The slippery slope

Matt's health was on the decline, and he soon required a blood transfusion before he started chemo. It was also discussed that he would need to visit the sperm bank before treatment commenced to preserve sperm for future use. This was a wake-up call to the toxic nature of chemotherapy. Throughout February 2015, Matt saw the pancreatic surgeon for an endoscopy, the neurosurgeon, endured more radiation therapy, had an appointment with the oncologist, received a blood transfusion, visited the sperm bank, and was told to see a member of the palliative care team for pain management. Every day there was a medical appointment, and every day he was looking worse. Travelling in and out of the hospitals in the city and on the North Shore was starting to wear us down. The daily trek was turning into a daily grind. If it was tiring for us, and we were able bodied, we knew it was exhausting for Matt.

Some hospitals are much nicer to visit than others and they have a more pleasant feel to them. The older hospitals have an eerie energy about them, and the rooms can feel dark and dingy, like a spooky castle with squeaky doors—like the sign our bedroom door was communicating. I am sure it was telling us Matt needed to be where positive energy abounds. It is not the type of place where one feels they can recuperate. The old convalescence type of hospital had it right, where they would take the patients out in to the garden to enjoy the fresh air, and the meals were home cooked and nutritious.

Chemotherapy commenced at the end of February, and Matt immediately reacted with a high temperature and visit to the emergency department on day one. His body reacted badly to the toxic cocktail that had entered his veins and in hindsight it may have been the reason we saw the abundance of blue violets signifying the extent of his blue veins being overwhelmed. We could see him fading away to a shell of himself. It was horrific to witness and even Matt was mortified when he saw his reflection in the mirror. All the while we were keeping up the IV vitamin C to give his body a chance. Three rounds of chemotherapy and three blood transfusions plus an iron infusion over three weeks nearly killed him. He lost twenty kilograms in eight weeks and was so weak he could barely walk. Martin was shocked when he saw him and immediately cancelled any further treatment. I believe that if it wasn't for the holistic regime that I had prescribed for Matt he would no longer be here with us.

The effect of chemotherapy on the body can be barbaric. Chemotherapy has been around for seventy years and very little has changed in that time. There is a standard dosing practice that is not suitable to everyone, and it has been proven overseas that smaller doses can work just as effectively without drastic side effects such as death. We understood that with uncommon and rare cancers the treatment options can be experimental as there have been no clinical trials to identify a treatment protocol. Matt was a guinea pig, and he very nearly lost his life.

One week later, Matt had another PET scan, and the results were appalling. The chemotherapy had destroyed his once robust immune system allowing the malignant cells to overcome his body. The cancer was now eating its way through his left shoulder and humorous, there were spots up and down his spine, and tumours through his pelvis, glutes, and quads. The PET scan lit up like the bright red Devils Dipsticks we found in the backyard, and naturally

Don't be Bitter be Better

Matt was devastated, yet it wasn't until a long time later that we divulged to him the horrible significance of this disturbing sign. This insidious disease (AMFH) was eating its way through Matt's body. A tumour that had appeared behind Matt's left knee was growing rapidly. We are not sure if that tumour was there from the outset, as the original PET scan did not go down to his knees. In retrospect this was a major oversight and would make us question whether this was the primary tumour, or just one metastasising from the spine.

> *"Our lives are not determined by what happens to us but how we react to what happens, not by what life brings us but the attitude we bring to life."*
> **Wade Boggs**

Matt had one of Australia's foremost authorities working his case, we were researching and doing everything within our power to keep him alive and to find the answer, but it didn't seem like it was enough. There had already been many medical mishaps along the way, and even though we had made informed, researched, and considered decisions based on scientific evidence, Matt still ended up with one foot in the grave. We did not endorse the idea of chemotherapy from the start and our research had shown that surgery and radiation were the better options, however, because of the aggressiveness of the disease and the previous bleeds spreading the cancer cells, there were no other options other than immunotherapy which was not yet available in Australia. It was time we took matters into our own hands, after all we wanted to have no regrets. We would throw everything conceivable at this challenge, including the daily reminder of keeping the "golden carrot" within sight.

Chapter 5

Slice and Dice

Matt was referred to yet another member of the dream team, a highly respected sarcoma surgeon, a larger-than-life imposing figure who came with a big reputation, and a huge workload. The tumours were stealing blood from Matt's circulation, and they needed to be removed. The pain in his shoulder and left arm were increasing as was the restriction of movement so it was decided that the shoulder would be reconstructed first by fitting a full prosthetic replacement. There was very little explanation of the procedure and little information given about the after-effects. He was advised he would no longer be able to swim using overarm, driving a manual car may be problematic, and the range of movement in that arm would be restricted. This was especially tough, as Matt was an avid swimmer. We had no idea just how restricted the arm would be until after the surgery. He would need a new car as his current model was a manual, raising his arm in a forward movement was no longer possible, and doing some simple tasks would prove extremely difficult. Matt just got on with the recovery process, and never complained. 'It is what it is' became his favourite saying, and the only way forward was to accept what is and move on.

All too often we would find ourselves sitting in the doctor's clinic thinking that everything was going along okay, until the doctor would ask Matt how he was. Often it would come out that Matt had concerns about another growth, or had pain, but had not disclosed it to us. He kept silent about aches and pains preferring not to be an alarmist as he did not want to worry us as he quietly pondered his condition until his next consultation. We would brace ourselves at each appointment waiting for another disease site to be disclosed. A major fricking headache (AMFH), was living up to its reputation. Talk about ground hog day!

His next surgery was scheduled for ten days after the left shoulder surgery. The surgery for his right leg was being performed at a different hospital to where he had the shoulder done, something to do with operating schedules and surgical team availability. The exponential growth of these tumours that were in his pelvis and right leg was frightening and somewhat akin to the movie alien. They seemed to virtually appear overnight and grew at such an expediated pace that they nearly took up the whole quad area of the leg. They needed to be removed quickly due to their ever-increasing size and the fact that they were taking blood from Matt's circulation, leaving him anaemic and weak. Due to the vascular nature of the tumours, a vascular surgeon was engaged to embolise and cut blood supply to the pelvic tumours which would decrease the risk of Matt haemorrhaging. This was to be routine surgery conducted just hours prior to him having major surgery on his right leg to remove damaged muscular tissue and tumours. He was in very good spirits before they wheeled him away to undergo the embolization procedure.

Slice and Dice

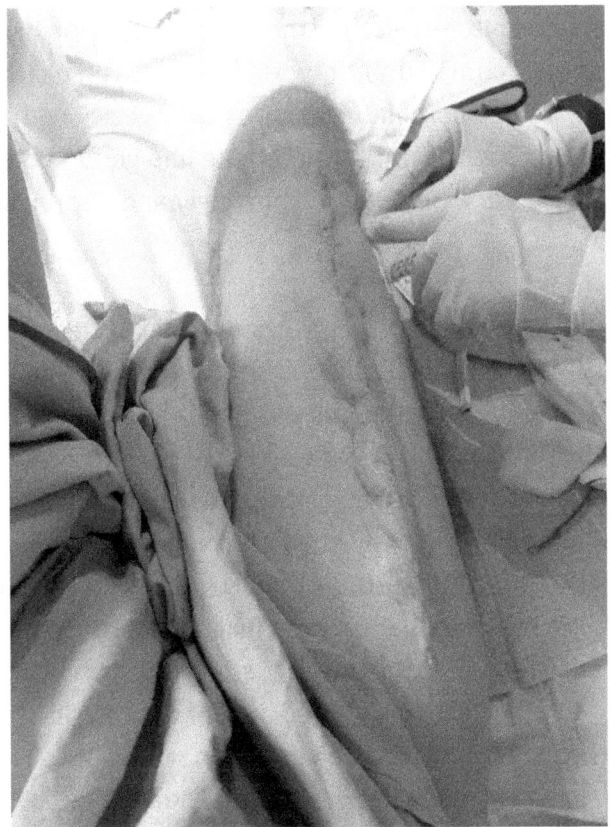

Matt's right thigh

Post recovery he was in agony with his right leg. He had severe pins and needles down the entire length of his leg, and he had no control of right-foot movement. This was one of the few times we saw Matt agitated and demanding answers. We questioned the nurses and they said it was probably the way that they had him lying during the surgery. After an hour it had not improved, it was worse, so we requested to see the vascular surgeon. He never arrived. We tried to get Matt up and walking to see if that would ease the pins and needles, but it did nothing to alleviate it. Several hours later they gave him stronger pain medication and he was wheeled into theatre for the major surgery on his leg. The dream team sarcoma surgeon was heading overseas for three weeks after he had completed the surgery. We relayed our fears to the sarcoma specialist that something had gone wrong during the vascular surgery, he nodded knowingly and disappeared into the theatre.

Matt looked like a victim of war. He had the left arm disabled, and supported in a sling, and his right leg semi paralysed with foot drop due to the vascular surgeon embolising his sciatic nerve in error. We were livid! Damaged nerves are very slow to heal and may regenerate at one millimetre per day, meaning it could take years to recover from the trauma if at all. He had been through enough already without this huge stuff up that was severely reducing his quality of life. That vascular surgeon failed to call or communicate and did not visit Matt in the hospital, so we called him. There was no apology for the damage incurred. Matt was prescribed a myriad of drugs to decrease the sciatic nerve pain, and to help him sleep. As he was in excruciating pain, emaciated and in a bad way, I rang Mick and advised him to come home as soon as possible, which he did. Mick got a hell of a shock when he saw Matt. From hiking and swimming in Hawaii to now, which was only five months, there was a massive decline in Matt's health. Mick stayed for one week to buoy Matt's spirits and to help where he could. This was wonderful not only for Matt but for all of us.

This medical error had just about destroyed any quality-of-life Matt had remaining. He was now unable to drive or walk any distance. On the positive side we were extremely thankful to all his friends that kept the constant vigil by his bed, making him laugh, and playing board games and cards with him. He had endured the ultimate torture and it was hell. Since returning eleven months earlier, he had been through nine surgeries, thirty-two rounds of radiation treatment and six rounds of chemotherapy. His dogged determination, strength of will, and the ability to smile and be happy was extraordinary.

> *"Our greatest glory is not in never falling,
> but in rising every time we fall."*
> **Confucius**

Following his release from hospital, Matt was booked in for group physiotherapy, plus individual sessions of exercise physiology. These programs helped to improve his stability and increased his muscle mass incrementally. Bit by bit, day by day, we would build a new version of Matt. As he said to his friends, "This is my new modified body." There was no anger, bitterness, or self-pity involved, he had a job to do. That job was to regain strength, mobility, and energy. Around this time, we started to look for novel treatments and spoke to practitioners both domestically and overseas to extend our awareness of emerging therapies.

We were advised of a sarcoma case where hyperthermia treatment had been used with some level of success. We were aware that there was one clinical trial unit in Sydney at that stage, and it was located at the back of RPA in an annex of Sydney University. We contacted the researcher who showed interest in Matt's case and was keen to give Matt the treatment. Matt's oncologist Martin was also on board with the hyperthermia treatment. We were elated that he was prepared to give this a go. However, the agreement fell over when the researcher announced to the oncologist that the only way Matt could use the machine would be for Martin to supervise a clinical trial with other patients. That was never going to happen as this was a one-off instance due to the rarity and complexity. A clinical trial involves enrolling a set number of patients with a similar disease state, then studying and recording the findings of the disease progression or regression. Some clinical trials can take years for them to be approved through an ethics committee. It was totally unrealistic for the researcher to request that Martin take on this role. It was a very disappointing outcome, and it highlighted the point that some people do not always value an individual's health over their own personal goals.

One month after the leg surgery we took Matt back to see the sarcoma surgeon. Matt was grey in skin tone, weak and noticeably underweight. As the surgeon looked at the latest PET scan, he stated that the malignant tumour behind Matt's left knee needed to be removed. I told him that was not going to happen right now. I knew that if Matt had any more surgery at this stage, it could kill him. He was too weak, and malignant tumour or not, we needed to rebuild him. We located a clinic in Queensland that was able to give Matt the hyperthermia treatment plus IV vitamin C, as at that stage there were none located locally. It was decided that I would take Matt for the initial treatments and set up a treatment protocol that I felt was appropriate for his condition and one that he was happy with. We booked him in for ten of these treatments, which now meant that we would be flying to Queensland every second week. Matt was very weak and unable to walk far at all, certainly not through the airport. He now needed wheelchair assistance to go any distance and the phrase, 'through adversity comes human resilience' kept entering my thoughts.

At age twenty-five, Matt had been pondering his own mortality which had been too close for comfort. We don't expect to be contemplating what happens to us if we die at a young age. It can be confronting and stressful, especially when one would think they had another seventy good years left in them to explore, love, and live well. Life can be tough, especially for the young who are ill and infirmed. We were now throwing everything we had at this dreadful disease including oncology services and integrative care, herbal medicine, targeted nutrition, IV vitamin C, hyperthermia, and hyperbaric treatment. In addition to the physical therapies, he was also having rehabilitation and we made sure that Matts social circle remained strong with his friends always being welcomed. A holistic treatment strategy that embodied mind, body and soul medicine was imperative to allow for healing. The focus being on the interactions of the brain, emotions and the body and the powerful ways in which emotional, mental, social, spiritual, and behavioural factors can directly affect health.

Ella arrives

It had now become quite evident that Matt would be spending some time with us whilst his body started to repair. From the time we had children, animals were a part of our family unit. We have had a variety of pets ranging from dogs, cats, fish, birds, and turtles, as we believed it was important for children to respect nature, and it teaches them responsibility. Animals are nonjudgmental, they are comforting in times of stress, they make great friends as you can tell them anything and they are usually cheerful. We were at that stage in life where we were enjoying more freedom, almost empty nesters, yet we knew a dog for Matt would be in his best interest during his recovery stage to bring him some joy and constant company. Matt wanted a rescue dog as he believed that every dog deserves a lovely home, and understandably from the time he commenced work he had donated part of his wage to the RSPCA.

After perusing the Sydney dog rescue shelters online Matt and Alex thought they had found a lovely dog which was cross a German Shepherd and Rottweiler. Alex and Matt drove one hour to the rescue shelter so they could inspect the dog. Alex liked it but Matt was not totally convinced. A few days later the three of us returned to the shelter. That dog was not the perfect fit but looking further up the row of cages I noticed a huge smile and glassy eyes intently looking at us. This dog's name was Ella, and she was very excited to see us with her pleading eyes conveying the take me home now message. We took her for a walk, and she was well behaved on the lead, with no pulling and she appeared low maintenance. She was a Wolfhound cross and a big girl at thirty kilograms. She had been dumped after having a litter of puppies and the owner had not returned the shelters phone calls. I could tell she had a lot of character and a big personality plus she was intelligent. She was an instant hit with the family when we brought her home.

Slice and Dice

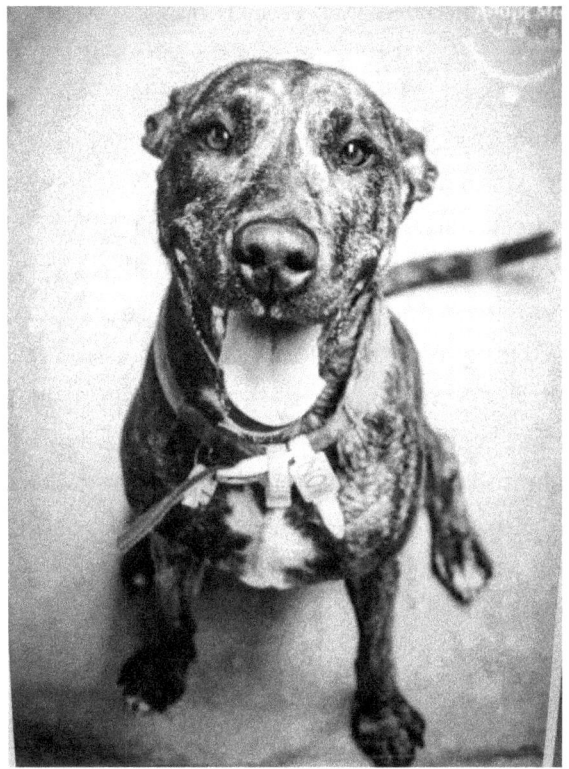

Ella

Ella was what the family needed. She brought happiness and a beautiful light energy to the household, she was very loving and cuddly, and was both Matt's and Alex's loyal companion. She was Matt's by day, and Alex's by night when he finished work. Ella's level of knowing and compassion with Matt was incredible. The adoration between them was palpable, and Ella was the perfect therapy and healing dog for Matt during his greatest time of need. She had her quirky ways and an eccentric personality that we had not previously witnessed in a dog, and although very unusual, this union was meant to be.

Don't be Bitter be Better

When she first came to live with us, I thought it best to take her to dog training. We would attend one night each week in a special class with the instructor barking out commands and enticing the dogs to obey with offers of treats. Ella was very easily distracted by all the other dogs and not motivated by food. We were unsure of her history but presumed she may have been trained for catching feral pigs, given her breed and speed. If any smaller dog came within reach, she would try to grab them and she seemed to think they were prey. One night in the middle of winter when I was training her, another dog went running past and she spun around to take off after it. She accelerated so fast she sent me flying off balance and I face planted into the grass, still holding onto the lead as she proceeded to drag me along. The instructor was shocked, and I laughed it off as I held on to her lead with a strong grip not daring to let go, it was lucky I wasn't hurt. Her lightning quick attack made us aware of her strength and determination to go after other dogs thus daytime walks were off the agenda. She has helped all of us to navigate some tricky times, to take our mind off destructive thoughts and to enjoy the pleasures of dog walking of a night. There is an old saying that says timing is of the essence. Ella's arrival was perfect timing for the times ahead. Ella is still alive today, but is getting old, she is one of the heroes of this story.

Chapter 6

One Door Closes

We had always had an open-door policy when the boys were growing up, and quite often the house was filled with extra people. It was the old analogy the more the merrier and when it came to Matt's social circle, this was something he excelled at. While in hospital there were a steady stream of friends by his bedside. This type of support was invaluable and kept him occupied and intrigued in life stories. When he was at home the house once more was filled with family and friends as he entertained people with stories from his travels or hilarious stories from his hospital stays. No matter how sick or tired he was feeling, he was always up for a game of cards or to challenge his friends to a board game. Some of his favourites being Cards Against Humanity, Secret Hitler, Munchkin, Dunbar, Blind Queens, and Spanish Eyes. There were many late afternoons when a group would rock up, set up and they played well into the night, with Matt's competitive spirit always planning to win.

Gradually, Matt was starting to claw his way back enabling me to take him for short walks, like just to the corner of our street which was slightly uphill. Although this was all he could manage, it was progress. Alex and Belle would take Matt out, either to a movie or to a restaurant which gave him an outing to look forward to, that didn't involve doctors, nurses, and hospitals. Our lives had revolved around appointments, hospital visits, meetings, rehab, and research, so it was incredibly important to have some balance, enjoy life and have fun. On our Queensland visits we were fortunate to have cousins living nearby who opened their house to us. We felt extremely welcomed at their generosity of cooking meals for us and keeping us company. We were also fortunate that a dear friend had offered her father's house for us to stay in. People's generosity and kindness was humbling. My hairdresser and long-time friend dropped meals around plus a huge box of fruit and vegetables. Close friends would take me out for a meal or a massage to give me a break. This level of support and kindness from friends and family was uplifting.

> *"One who gains strength by overcoming obstacles possesses the only strength which can overcome adversity."*
> **Albert Schweitzer (1875-1965)**

Nearly one year on from when Matt was first diagnosed it was time for another PET scan. The scan showed multiple disease sites including in his neck, lower spine, femur, legs, and pelvis. Martin was at his wits end and suggested a different type of chemo at a lower dose and Matt agreed to trying this. At the same time, we had found a professor in Melbourne whom we thought may have been able to view Matt's case with a fresh set of eyes and assist Matt with his integrative health program. His speciality was treating cancer patients by combining evidence-based complementary therapies with conventional medicine. Although we were already doing this, I felt another opinion would be of benefit and perhaps he could offer further suggestions. Matt was quite feeble when we decided to fly to Melbourne for a day to see what this professor could offer. I had already briefed the professor on both mine and David's background and advised him of our extensive biochemical, nutritional, counselling, and naturopathic knowledge in addition to the range of treatments Matt had already tried. We felt like everything we said fell on deaf ears as we sat in his clinic for over two hours. During those two hours, we listened to him go through diet, lifestyle, emotional health, and he then proceeded to show Matt on his iPad how he could be gardening! This academic appeared to be a one trick pony, what a waste of time and money.

I felt like he paid no attention to my brief, our expertise or to Matt. It was like he had a set script, and agenda and he would not sway from it. We could see Matt gradually wilting in the chair, in pain and uncomfortable after sitting there for over two hours. This was even more confirmation to trust ourselves, our training, and our knowledge to get the job done for Matt.

Every second day in June 2015 Matt had an appointment with either a specialist, physio- rehab or to have treatment. He underwent a further three rounds of chemo which knocked him around, although thankfully not as brutal as the first course. During July and August, we were still flying frequently to Queensland for IV vitamin C and hyperthermia treatments, and in Sydney he had appointments with the sarcoma surgeon, and Martin the oncologist. Matt underwent another PET scan in August, followed a few days later by the usual post scan briefing. Martin was usually quite jovial and enjoyed telling stories of his travels overseas. This appointment was different, as he sat stony faced and pushed the written summary of the PET results across the desk towards Matt. It was like one of those scenes in a movie where you didn't need to know the content, it was written on his face. He gently informed us, "I regret to say that there is nothing else we can do. We have run out of options. Is there anything else I can do to help you?"

Don't be Bitter be Better

This was another massive blow and shock, beyond belief. Matt was silent, and all I could think of was, that the answer was out there somewhere, and we would find it. It seemed unbelievable that a fit, young man with the world at his feet could end up in this position through no fault of his own. It seemed inconceivable that he had endured six chemotherapy treatments, thirty-two rounds of radiation, nine surgeries, six hyperthermia treatments, ten IV vitamin C's, months of rehab, all in the space thirteen months for this outcome. The glass half empty approach would have felt like all that pain and suffering was for nothing. We are half full people, and we had our son and was determined to keep him that way. Only later did we realise what a pivotal moment in Matt's battle had we just then experienced.

The world is a big place and there are some amazing medical milestones being reached in cancer treatments. We just needed to find the right place, which seemed like finding a needle in a haystack. With the three of us researching daily I felt confident that we would indeed find the right place. One night in August, I had finished work quite late, it was dark, and I was walking up the front stairs to our house. As I was thinking about Matt and the predicament he was in when this loud, booming voice came out of nowhere and said, "It's time!" It scared the hell out of me as there was no one else around. I quietly asked, "It's time now?" "Yes, do it now." The universe had spoken and who was I to ignore such wisdom. David and Matt were in Queensland, and Alex was at work. I had just been told in no uncertain terms it was now or never. I dropped my bags as I walked through the front door and went straight to the computer to look at my previous searches for the best clinic in the world for Matt.

> *"Decisiveness is a characteristic of high-performing men and women. Almost any decision is better than no decision at all."*
> **Brian Tracy**

We had previously called doctors in clinics in Europe, America and Mexico, and searched clinics in Asia and the UK looking for the right place. Google searching can be full of misrepresentations and there seemed to be a lot of unorthodox and unethical clinics preying on the weak, dying, and vulnerable. I have a very good BS (bullshit) meter, as does Matt, so this whittled down the list of viable options. David made many phone calls along the way, which helped cull many of the options we had been looking at. One night, after work when I was searching, I noticed on the sidebar that a clinic came up advertising second generation and monoclonal antibody treatment options amongst other things. The more I looked the more excited I became. What Matt needed to get him through this was a novel, futuristic, targeted, personalised treatment, and I felt this was a clinic that could deliver. I rang Matt and David immediately, although it was now 10pm. David recognised the clinic as one that he had short listed from his researching, so Matt read their bio and it was agreed to email them immediately as it was during office hours in Germany. Our intuition proved sound as we spoke to the clinic director and immediately felt assured that this was survival central for those that pharmaceutical medicine had failed.

The power of intention

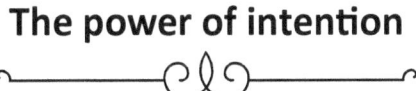

In a leap of faith, I rang Qantas that night and booked fares for Matt and myself to travel to Germany. I used all our frequent flyer points hoping to get Matt a business class fare, but they were already booked out. I told Karen, the contact at Qantas of our predicament and that I needed to get my sick son to Germany urgently, and that he would need to lie down as he was too weak to remain seated for twenty-three hours.

She said that there was one first-class seat available that I could use the points for, and I could fly economy. They were the last seats on the plane. What a blessing, I could hardly believe our luck. The fares were booked, we were going in a few weeks' time, and now I had a timeline to work with. I also knew that if I did not get Matt there soon, his time would run out. Now we needed to book him into the clinic, book the accommodation, plus a car, and train tickets. Nothing was too difficult except for the foreign language barrier, which we mastered eventually.

The senior physician at the clinic was extremely generous with his time. We had emailed all Matt's scan results, pathologies and treatments conducted so far. The clinic would conduct their own pathology testing to identify immunotherapy options or other treatments that were not available in Australia. All of this came at an exorbitant price, but what price do you place on your child's life? During the next three weeks before our trip we had a lot to get organised. We spoke to Martin and told him what we were proposing. He knew the clinic and he knew of their work but said that the treatment was not available in Australia. His hands were tied, but he said he would do what he could to help us get there. We went with his blessing. He organised for the lab at RPA to release the pathology slides of Matt's tumour and package them for me to take. He also wrote a letter to the specialist at the German clinic, and he wrote a letter giving medical clearance for Matt to travel. Martin was instrumental in helping us with all the bureaucracy.

Matt had one more trip up to Queensland for IV and hyperthermia treatments before we left for Germany, and it was there that we hatched a funding plan. After receiving the initial quote from the German clinic, we knew that we would need financial assistance to get through this. We had already thrown a lot of resources at treatments in Australia to help get him through but heading overseas, this was a whole new ballgame. The performing arts teachers at the high school that Matt had attended heard of his predicament and within two weeks they had organised a benefit concert to help Matt get to Germany. This was an amazing night, with the performance band playing, dancers, singers, and the school ensemble, all donating their time to raise money. The school hall was packed, and the generosity of the Engadine High community was incredible. The teaching staff that organised it put in a huge effort for which we are extremely grateful.

Matt also started up a crowd fundraising page. We have never asked for or expected financial assistance of any kind, so to ask people to donate was really stepping outside of our comfort zone. We learnt to gratefully accept all sorts of donations and many from people who could've done with donations themselves. The generosity of strangers, friends, Matt's workmates, and the company he works for was amazing. My brother and brother-in-law assisted financially, as did a friend who has struggled all her life as a single mum. She handed me a bag of cash that her father had bequeathed her and told me to use it. She said she would hate to be in my predicament and if she was, she would not know what to do. My closest friend, Dee, drew against her mortgage to lend me the cost of the initial quote at the clinic. This was a very large sum of money but without her assistance I would have needed to arrange substantial borrowings from our bank before we left, and I was running out of time. She knew she could trust me to pay her back when I had organised the funds with the bank. There were so many people that assisted us financially and emotionally to get Matt to that clinic. I was convinced it was meant to be.

> *"The world is a looking glass and gives back to every man the reflection on his own face."*
> **William Makepeace Thackery (1811-1863)**

Daily Fresh Juice Recipe

Use fresh produce only. It is best purchased organically or from a farmers market if possible.

- ½ beetroot
- 2 stalks of celery
- 2 carrots
- ½ lemon with the skin on
- 1 x apple
- Pineapple
- Small amount of ginger

To change it around you can add a cucumber or a small amount of watermelon.

This recipe aids in digestion, builds the blood and strength, helps with the immune system and gives the person "live" food to improve energy levels.

Chapter 7

Another Door Opens

As we headed into Sydney airport with Matt in a wheelchair the reality of the situation was hard to ignore. I now had the samples of Matt's tumour in my handbag, and I was trusting that my bag would not be snatched by an unwitting thief. Of all the thoughts to go through my head this was a major concern, because if that happened the German lab would not be able to match a treatment for Matt and this trip would be in vain. Compounding the stress levels, I was also concerned at the check-in as Matt was looking like the character Golem from The Lord of the Rings. The airport staff inquired if he could walk and what was the matter with him. I replied, "Yes, he could walk a little bit, certainly enough to take his seat once on the plane." Luckily, we had the medical certificate from Martin clearing Matt for flying, as without it I feel sure that the airline would have refused boarding. He was at death's door and I'm sure blind Freddy could've seen that. He had to get on that plane as this was his last chance, and we all knew it. If something were to happen on the flight or in Germany at least I would be there by his side, and I would feel comforted that we had done everything humanly possible to save his life.

"Go for it now. The future is promised to no one."
Wayne Dyer

Don't be Bitter be Better

My life motto is *no regrets*, and two of Matt's favourite sayings is *go hard or go home*, and *don't be bitter be better*. I am a firm believer in doing what is needed and what you feel in your heart is right, for the betterment of yourself and mankind, therefore having no regrets. Along the way there had been many questions by well-meaning people as to why we were taking Matt overseas and away from the healthcare in Australia and why we were spending so much money on treatment. I hope those people find the answers in this story. There were also the gossip mongers and negative nellies questioning Matt's myriad of treatments, and the notion of seeking overseas treatment gave them a lot to talk about. Unfortunately, there were people who took things to the next level. These were few and far between, thank goodness, however, I had someone verbally harass and threaten me, telling me that I was a piece of shit. This verbal attack almost led me to taking out a restraining order. The level of aggression and harassment at that time, from someone whom I had deemed as close shocked both me and my family. It just goes to show that whilst most people are supportive when there is a crisis, there are some people that look to drag others down. Symbolic of the Eastern philosophy of Yin and Yang.

Matt was interviewed by our local newspaper, attracting awareness to his story and with that came a lot of support as well as some judgment. Oh, to be condemnatory. I suppose in today's media savvy population, there will be the trolls and mud raking, but in my experience, people are pessimistic and judgemental because of their own insecurities, and it's easier to judge others instead of looking at themselves. For the most part this was like water off a duck's back, I had no time for negativity, only positivity, and I was determined that this was going to be a positive outcome. I was 99.5% sure of it. There definitely was that half a per cent of doubt that crept into my thoughts occasionally, but I refused to give that notion any oxygen.

Another Door Opens

New adventures

When we finally boarded the plane, I felt a huge sigh of relief. We were on our way, and we were both cautiously excited. Matt turned left and upstairs, upon entering the plane. He had his own little cubicle, his own bed, a bathroom, and a personal chef. There was also a large bar area that was stocked with lots of yummy snacks that one could help themselves to. I was seated downstairs in economy, and I was so elated and hyped up about this trip that I didn't sleep. I must admit I did spend some time upstairs with Matt in his own little oasis. Flying first class you can even have a shower at 30,000 feet. It was a unique way to fly first class, but perhaps it would be more fun under different circumstances.

Upon arriving at Munich, we checked into our hotel for one night's good sleep before embarking on a further day of travelling to the clinic. The clinic was located within a semi-rural area adjacent to Germany's Black Forest. Our travels commenced at Munich train station which is massive by Australian standards. We were to get the train from Munich to Stuttgart which would take a few hours. I knew some German language, but my vocabulary was not strong. Trying to order food for Matt and myself was proving to be hilarious. I resorted to charades and pretending to be a chicken to order a chicken salad. We noticed at the train station there were a lot of refugees coming through. We were there at the time when the refugees were coming across the German borders and seeking asylum. The country train that we had booked our seats on was completely full of fleeing migrants.

Once at Stuttgart it was challenging. I had booked a car and needed to find the booking office which was located within the station. This station was enormous and the walk to the office was about 300 metres. Juggling our luggage and backpack, this was a struggle by any stretch, and I was also keeping a close eye on Matt who was looking paler by the minute. When we finally reached the office, Matt was looking dreadful and they had no seating available, and proceeded to tell me that the car was a further half kilometre away in an underground car park. There was no way that Matt would make it. I had to request a chair for Matt and leave him in the office with all the bags whilst I went in search of the car.

Upon locating the vehicle, I needed to navigate a bustling city to find the concourse exit near where I had left Matt to pick him up. It would have been easy to panic at that point, driving on the wrong side of the road and hoping I was heading in the right direction and praying that Matt was still upright when I got back. Keeping my wits about me, being present and breathing, I managed to park in a small waiting bay outside the door where Matt was waiting. I threw the bags into the car and Matt navigated our way onto the Autobahn. The German Autobahn is a multi laned highway that has no speed limit for the most part, or conditional minimal limits enabling cars to travel up to 300 kilometres per hour. I had always wanted to drive on the Autobahn, but I never thought I would be doing it under these circumstances. It was nerve-racking at first with cars whizzing by doing more than 200 kilometres per hour, and what an experience. Initiation by fire! I was on a mission, and this was all part of the experience. Driving through the beautiful countryside in autumn was blissful. We went past many gorgeous little towns, beautiful green pastures, and quaint cottages.

Another Door Opens

Day 1. Matt at Lake Mummelsee

It was mid-afternoon when we finally arrived in the village of Hallwang, our destination. We made it, we made it to the Magic Castle. Following check-in, Matt was quickly seen by a doctor who advised us of the treatment schedule, which would commence the following day. I had booked our accommodation at a house two blocks away from the private hospital. It was a typical German house, built to withstand the cold and our two-bedroom flat was located upstairs. It was a very pretty, little country town with horses in paddocks, one supermarket and this amazing private oncology clinic. We were told to arrive at 9am the next day for Matt to see the doctor and be prepared to commence his prescribed treatment.

The day of deliverance had arrived. As I handed over the precious tumour slides for their lab to investigate, Doctor N and Doctor Z introduced themselves, showed us into their office and started asking a barrage of questions. This was the baseline, how was Matt, how is his energy, how did he manage the travelling halfway across the globe. They were internationally trained with near perfect English. Doctor N became the educator reaching for his black marker pens and butchers' paper and started writing and drawing diagrams and talking very fast and excitedly. Everything was spelt out clearly, including what they were proposing to start with, and how long it may take to get the results back from the lab. Matt's tumour sample and bloods would be tested to find the best prescription worldwide. Depending on the lab results they proposed to use a combination of next generation medicine, including antibody treatment, antigen treatment, immunotherapy, IV vitamin C and whatever else was required. This treatment plan was at the forefront of cancer treatments worldwide. Immediately they took blood from Matt and sent him into a treatment room. This was a very large room set up with recliner chairs and IV bags. Most of the chairs were occupied when we walked in.

All the staff were compassionate and friendly, and they immediately set up an IV for Matt to improve his energy levels, his digestion and give him a bit of strength. They also made up a drink called Fresubin which helped patients put on weight and improved energy levels. The staff were attentive with the patients, everything was checked twice a day, including bloods, temperature, hydration, food intake and bowels. From the minute we walked in the door Matt's health was attended to immediately. There was no waiting for days or weeks for anything to happen. Although we are incredibly thankful that we live in such a great country, we had been very frustrated with the health system in Australia. When someone has an aggressive metastatic cancer, they do not have time to wait for delays in treatment. These people need to be treated immediately otherwise the cancer will march through the body, as we had seen firsthand.

> *"If you want to succeed you should strike out on new paths, rather than travel the worn paths of accepted success."*
> **John D. Rockefeller**

Another Door Opens

In this private hospital in the middle of the German countryside there were people from many different countries. This was a medical mecca. We met people from Australia, France, UK, New Zealand, Ireland, Scotland, Estonia, America, and Italy. There were people from all walks of life but the one thing they had in common was that they were given no hope by the medical profession in their own country. Most had already undergone chemotherapy, radiation and surgery and had turned up here as their last chance. Compared to how Matt looked at that stage, most of them looked comparatively healthier. It was an eye-opening experience and everyday Matt and I would go to the treatment room and meet someone new and find out their story. Some people would come to the clinic every six months to get a top up to keep them well. One woman with an aggressive breast cancer had been doing this for the last four years. She had young children and she wanted to make sure that she lived long enough to see them as adults. Most had lived well past the predictions of their doctors, only because of the treatment they were receiving at this clinic.

Hallwang Clinic

Don't be Bitter be Better

Matt had been there for approximately four days when we noticed a man coming in on a stretcher, with doctors working on him and his two big burly sons following. He was from one of the Eastern Bloc countries and was flown in by air ambulance. His cells were haemorrhaging inside, and he had been told he had less than twenty-four hours to live and that his sons needed to make arrangements. When he arrived at the clinic, he was unconscious and in a very bad way. The next day when we turned up in the treatment room the two sons were there with their father. He didn't look too well, however he was conscious, but still unable to communicate or feed himself. The following day the colour started coming back into his face and he was starting to talk to his sons. We could see he was starting to recover; it was like looking at the living dead. A few days later I went for a walk in the Black Forest, and as I exited, here was the man with his two sons walking down the street. This was nothing short of a miracle and it happened before our eyes. It was an incredible recovery, Dr N and Dr Z had stopped the haemorrhaging in his cells and placed him on a treatment program which saw him not only fully recover but thrive. He stayed at the clinic for three weeks, and then he flew back home and went back to work running his own business. This reinforced in our minds that it is never too late to seek the correct treatment. There was a lot of hope and a lot of positivity at this hospital.

"I am not a product of my circumstances
I am a product of my decisions."
Stephen Covey (1932-2012) – Educator, Author, Businessman

Chapter 8

The Master Plan

It was September 2015 and whilst the days were warm, there was a coolness in the air and the night times were chilly. The flat we rented was somewhat old, but it had double glazed windows, heated floors, and oil heaters in every room. Each morning before Matt was due at the clinic, I would get up early and go for a walk through the town, knowing I would be sitting with him most of the day. There were apple trees lining the road, the odd horse in the paddocks, cigarette machines on the side of the road and a stillness that was quite peaceful. Across the road from the clinic was the Black Forest which went up into the mountains. The pine trees were huge and close together, the forest itself was quite dark, due to minimal sunlight penetrating through the thickness of the foliage.

At the entrance to the forest was a track called the Barefoot Forest Walk. There was an experiential short walk that people could take without their shoes on, just to feel the soft carpet of pine needles. It was an interesting concept especially coming from Australia where many people just wear thongs or no shoes at all. Quite often after lunch when Matt needed to rest, I would go for a walk through the forest for about an hour. Even though it was beautiful I also felt somewhat on edge as it was a lot darker and denser than our forests back home. I did not have a map of the tracks and there was no internet connection available in the forest. I was also concerned about wildcats and boars, and hoping there was no mass murderer, past or present, lurking in that forest. This was of course an unsubstantiated fear brought on by watching cold case files and murder mysteries. Each time I walked the tracks I rarely saw a soul, but it was good just to clear my head and inhale the fresh cool mountain air.

> *"When it is dark enough you can see the stars."*
> **Ralph Waldo Emerson (1803-1882)**

One day Matt was admitted into a room upstairs so he could lie down in a bed. The doctors discovered he was haemorrhaging from his cells, and he needed a transfusion urgently. I had just left the room to walk in the forest, and Matt had risen out of bed to use the bathroom. The cannula came flying out of his arm and blood was going everywhere. He tried to call me in a panic, but I had no reception. By the time the nurse came in the blood was all up the walls and all over the floor and the room looked like a murder scene. The language barrier prevented him from explaining how the situation arose and he felt quite shaken by the graphic nature of the event.

Each day there would be a meeting with either Dr N or Dr Z to discuss blood test results and preliminary pathology findings. It was decided that Matt would start on antigen treatments as the lab results would soon be available. These results would give a percentage rating for the efficacy of the treatment against his type of cancer. I could see he was already starting to look better; his appetite had increased, and his energy had improved slightly with the treatments he had already been given.

During our second week there, Mick arrived by train, a slower transport option that wouldn't have been suitable for Matt but probably less stressful than Autobahn driving. I was very glad to see him and thankful he was able to take time off work, and grateful he made the effort to be with his twin and myself. Mick is quite the comedian and having him there made a huge difference to Matt's mental well-being. Mick sat by Matt's side whilst he underwent treatment, he joked with him, stirred him up, diffused the tenseness of the situation and tried to smash everyone at cards. It didn't seem to matter how sick Matt was, it was nearly impossible to defeat him at any game requiring memory and strategy.

Depending on what time Matt would be released from the clinic he often returned to the flat so he could sleep and recover, and I would drive to a nearby town. Mick and I visited many of the little country towns and particularly enjoyed exploring the friendliness and warmth of the cobblestoned town squares. Matt decided one day he needed a haircut and Mick quickly volunteered to do this for him. He should have known that if his prankster brother decided to volunteer his prowess with the shears it would mean trouble. So, with clippers in hand and taking advantage of Matt not having any energy to retaliate, a chuckling Mick shaped Matt's unruly do in to a mohawk, much to Matt's horror. It did give us all a good laugh though, until Mick finally got round to reshaping it.

Don't be Bitter be Better

Playing mini golf with Mohawk

On another occasion Mick and I took Matt across the road where there was a mini golf course. Matt was unsteady on his feet with very little energy, but he still gave it a go. Here was a game that we could finally whip him at, as it did not rely on memory or strategy. It was good to see him with Mick outside in the fresh air having fun, plus this was a different type of challenge, but still one where he wanted to beat us. Every day that Matt was having treatment we would eat lunch at the clinic, these were beautifully prepared nutritious home cooked meals that were catered exclusively to your tastes. Of an evening I would visit the local supermarket and purchase supplies to cook dinner back at the flat. This had its own challenges as quite often I could not tell what type of protein I was purchasing as everything was written in German. I needed to scan most of the purchases with my phone to translate to English, however by the time we left Hallwang I was skilled at supermarket shopping in Germany.

Every day at the clinic was full on. There would be more testing, IV infusions, or blood transfusions, but at least something was happening every single day. Juggling this with keeping David up to date, attending to all my work emails and running the two businesses remotely, plus keeping the rest of the family and friends up to speed was trying. Personally, this was exhausting, but I used my brave face to make it all look easy although it was not. I started to miss the small things about home, like the sound of the magpies, kookaburras, and the hum of the bees on the flowers, noises that would wake me up every morning and now in this small country town there was just silence. We had gone from an abundance of wildlife and fauna to virtually nothing, not even a bird song. I missed Ella, David, and Alex, and I missed our variety of freshly picked fruit and vegetables. There was no point feeling down about it, it was a matter of biting the bullet, getting through it, and feeling thankful we made it to this amazing mecca.

Unleash success

Finally, the lab results arrived, and Matt was summonsed to Dr N's office. Out came the butchers' paper again, as he excitedly penned the plan of action. There were two different treatment types that Matt's cancer had responded positively too. Neither was a perfect match, they were both below 50%, however if combined it would give the effect of nearly 100% efficacy. Like most medications they had side effects that could not be avoided but the potential gain far outweighed the negatives. Dr N had taken measurement of the tumour behind Matt's left knee when we arrived. This tumour was enormous and pronounced so that any change due to treatment effects could easily be observed. Finally, we had a targeted therapy to use for Matt. The clinic ordered the treatment and Matt was ready to commence an entirely new form of tumour attack.

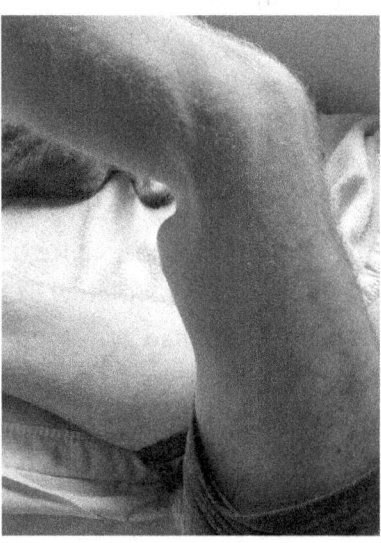

The tumour behind Matt's knee

The Master Plan

We had been given an estimate of treatment costs before heading over to Germany and this was around €60,000. The invoice for the first two weeks was A$120,000 as this included $20,000 for the laboratory matching, antigen and antibody therapies, blood testing and transfusion, and other therapies. This was way above what I was expecting it to be and came as a bit of a shock. Thank goodness we had done some fundraising before we left to help cover some of it.

Whilst waiting for the treatment vials to arrive we decided we would drive over the Alps across the border into France to sightsee the city of Strasbourg. As we wound our way through the mountains of the Black Forest we stopped at little villages along the way, eventually arriving at the mountain summit. The three of us got out of the car as the scenery was remiss of the sound of music. It was both breathtaking and exhilarating, plus it ticked the box of being soul food for not only Matt but also for Mick and me. It was just a one-day adventure, but it took us into a different country and culture and allowed us to explore away from the clinic and medical intervention. Matt handled the day very well and we could see a change for the better in his health.

Finally, the treatment arrived, and Dr N and Dr Z then needed to calculate an appropriate dose that would shrink the tumours, cease the internal bleeding, and halt any further growths, without jeopardising Matt's life. All treatments have side effects, and this one did too. The antigen treatment that he had already started on had primed his body and his cells so they would uptake this next treatment quickly. It was decided that he would have six of these treatments, which would need to be at least three to five days apart, depending on his blood results and liver pathology. One of the side effects of the treatment was high temperatures, and that needed to be monitored very closely. Matt needed to be booked into a private hospital room to have these treatments administered. After having the first treatment Matt did have a high temperature, headache, body aches and pains.

The doctors at the clinic prefer patients not to take paracetamol to reduce the temperature as this can affect the treatment outcome. With each treatment round the side effects would increase. His legs became weak and felt very heavy, the headaches more severe and the lethargy increased. The flat that we had rented was upstairs on the first floor, and Matt was having a lot of difficulty walking up those stairs. It took him ages just to walk up twelve stairs, and by the time he got to the top he was exhausted. One day when he was lying in bed at the apartment, he experienced an excruciating pain in his neck and was temporarily paralysed with fear of movement. To me this was not looking good, but Matt who overcame his concerns braced himself without moving his neck and managed to sit up. His neck would prove to be difficult for the remainder of the trip. We were unsure whether this to was an unwanted side effect of the treatment, as he had so much going on with his body it was hard to differentiate one ache or pain from another.

> *"There is no such thing as a hopeless situation. Every single circumstance of your life can change!"*
> **Rhonda Byrne – Author of The Secret**

Back at the clinic, the doctors were very excited after the first two treatments as Matt's bloodwork had improved, and the tumour behind his knee was starting to shrink. He was still having the other IV therapies in the common treatment room daily and had started to see the physiotherapist at the clinic for exercises to build strength. After ten days of being with Matt and myself, Mick was heading off to party at Oktoberfest in Munich for a few days, then he was flying back to Tokyo. He kept us entertained with photos of himself clowning around dressed up in traditional Bavarian lederhosen. When I originally booked our accommodation and airfares to go to Germany, I thought we would be there for three weeks, however at the three-week mark Matt was still undergoing treatment. We ended up being there for a total of five weeks. I had taken over a large supply of supplements and herbal formulas that I had been dispensing to Matt, but I had only taken enough for approximately twenty-eight days, which now meant I had to ration supplies to last the distance. Some being better than none.

Matt had the six immunotherapy treatments as planned, the tumour behind his knee had shrunk and the doctors explained that these immunotherapy treatments keep working in the body to kill the cancer cells. They explained that Matt would need to come back for further treatment within a few months. Towards the end of that five weeks Matt and I drove once more over the mountains and into Strasbourg to meet Alexaine, a friend of Matt's. She had travelled six hours by train from Nice to meet Matt and have lunch together. Matt had offered her accommodation in Santiago when she had nowhere else to go and was feeling quite destitute. She stayed in his spare room until she found work and her own accommodation. She had kept in contact all this time. She spoke of Matt's kindness, offering her somewhere to stay, and said it was funny as she immediately trusted him and could see he was a good person. It was lovely that she made the effort to travel to Strasbourg to spend some time with Matt.

On our last day in clinic as we settled the bill and gave thanks, we were both relieved to finally be heading back home. Matt was in much better shape than when we had arrived, he had put on weight, his colour looked better, his appetite had improved, and he had more energy. The final bill was astronomical by our Aussie standards, but these doctors and nurses had saved Matt's life. As we hopped back on the Autobahn heading towards Munich, we took a detour as we could see this massive Cathedral in a town called Münster. This was one of the biggest cathedrals I had ever seen and certainly the biggest for Matt. It was awe inspiring and I lit a candle to give thanks and to shine a light on Matt's health. Whilst we were in Germany my sister and her husband had trekked the Camino Trail (Spain) and along the way had stopped at many churches to light a candle for Matt. Another friend, Jo, was also travelling overseas and visited cathedrals to light a few candles for Matt. Back in Australia a friend's brother who worked with the order of nuns had asked them all to pray for Matt. So many people had prayed, sent him good wishes, and wanted him to be well, and I feel that all this positive energy found its way to Matt and helped him in more ways than one. It takes a village to raise a child and it certainly took a global village to assist Matt and to navigate our way through this.

We finally arrived in Munich where we would spend two nights before boarding our flight back home. The following day was Matt's birthday, and he was turning twenty-six. I decided we would eat lunch at the Crowne Plaza in Munich. It was a one block walk from our hotel, and, amazingly, Matt was able to walk it. We had a lovely seafood lunch and then headed back to the hotel to rest before our trip. On the return flight Matt was booked on business class so he had a bed, and I was in economy again. Before we had left the clinic, Dr N had suggested that there were two drugs that were new to the market that he thought Matt should be taking. The cost of these tyrosine kinase inhibitor drugs combined would be $17,000 per month. I had purchased a one-month supply from him and would get the rest in Australia. I also had marijuana oil that he had prescribed to help with the appetite, some strong enzymes, low dose chemo tablets and a list of other suggestions. This time I didn't have a tumour in my handbag, I had a handbag full of drugs.

> *"In every success story, you find someone
> who has made a courageous decision."*
> **Peter F. Drucker**

Arriving back in Sydney I felt an enormous sense of relief that we had both survived this challenging trip, with encouraging results. We had a master plan in place now, one that was clearly working. Matt continued with the regime I had implemented plus the program that Dr N and Dr Z had recommended. I was back at work the next day attempting to catch up on tasks that arose in my absence and seeing clients. At Matt's next appointment with Martin, he was amazed that the tumour behind Matt's knee was no longer visible. Matt's bloodwork had improved and overall, he was looking better than before we left for Germany. The previous appointment with Martin had been in August, and it was now late October, the transformation was incredible. Over the next few weeks Matt started to put on weight, his appetite increased, and he was able to move about more freely and socialise with friends. We decided Matt and David would head back to Hallwang for three weeks in December for the next round of treatment.

The second trip was a totally different experience than the first, as everything had already been set up for them. Once again, Matt needed to fly business class and the airline kindly upgraded David for the first leg of the flight. The apartment they stayed in was right next to the hospital, which ended up being a blessing. They were there during Germany's winter, and although not snowing it was icy and extremely cold. Dr N could feel the tumour behind Matt's knee beginning to grow and it was decided that he would dose Matt with Ektomon Anti-GD2 a targeted immunotherapy using monoclonal antibodies. Monoclonal antibodies are lab-made versions of immune system proteins that can attach to a specific target on the cells in the body. These antibodies can be injected into the blood to seek out and attach to cancer cells. This time around it was decided the treatments would be closer together and at a higher dose, as Dr N felt that Matt's condition would deteriorate otherwise. He hoped that Matt's body would be able to handle the treatment.

Chapter 9

Bring It On!

Matt had been diagnosed with a cancer so rare that there were only a few reported cases worldwide. During Matt's second visit to Germany, I was busy trying to juggle the responsibilities of both work and home, plus attempting to raise more funds for the treatment that Matt required. It arose during a discussion with Martin about the exorbitant cost of the tyrosine kinase inhibitors, that he suggested I contact the directors of a new charity that had commenced specifically to help people with rare cancers.

Unfortunately, for anyone with a rare cancer diagnosis there is minimal public awareness and little or no funding available for assistance with treatment. Most cancer charities raise money for well-known and much publicised cancers such as breast, prostate, and bowel cancer. This leaves a whopping 30% of the population who have been diagnosed with a rare cancer unfunded. We had attempted to access a government grant for people who need to travel overseas to have treatment. Matt's case was knocked back due to the absence of researched data on his cancer type with the consequence being a lack of established treatment protocols. The irony of it was that this grant was there to help people like Matt to obtain treatments that were only available overseas, but you had to prove their efficacy. The literature is there now because he has had a few doctors write research papers about him.

> *"Strength does not come from physical capacity.*
> *It comes from an indomitable will."*
> **Mahatma Gandhi**

In December 2015 I rang Kate Vines, one of the directors of Rare Cancers Australia. I explained Matt's case, the position we were in, and the expected ongoing cost of the inhibitors he had been prescribed. Kate was warm and sincere and completely familiar with the frustration brought about by the lack of support available to rare cancer patients. The fact that someone absolutely understood the financial strain was enormously comforting. This was a kindred spirit who not only knew what we were going through but more importantly she knew how to lobby for patient care, she is a person of much integrity.

She said she would talk to the pharmaceutical company that supplied the inhibitors and see if she could arrange for compassionate access. Kate rang the next day and said that they had come to the party for one month. This woman was an angel who came at exactly the right time when we needed the support. Kate also suggested starting a fundraising page for Matt through Rare Cancers Australia (RCA). Kate and her husband, Richard, kindly donated to Matt's fund to kickstart it. This would be the start of an enduring relationship with an amazing couple.

No one person has all the answers, meaning; look outside of the current circle of practitioners. This slice of wisdom came from a complete stranger, who suggested Matt seek a second opinion from a senior sarcoma specialist in Sydney. This was arranged and we were excited to discuss the success of the treatment Matt had in Germany. To our surprise, he was dismissive of the overseas treatment and failed to offer any other treatment options Matt could try. He politely concluded the consultation with the summation that Matt's condition would continue to progress unabated. Another negative experience chalked up. Martin on the other hand was completely supportive and never disputed the efficacy of next generation medicine.

After Matt had arrived home from his second trip to Germany, we had a steady stream of visitors to the house to check on his progress. He was exhausted from the treatment and the trip, and even though he had improved, his physical appearance was still confronting. A family friend came to visit and whilst she held it together with Matt, once she stepped outside she was visibly shaken and crying and asked if he was going to make it? She also stated that Matt had always been very lucky, whatever he touched turned out a success. Then she inquired, had Matt been cursed? I had wondered the same thing earlier on, who had stabbed him in the back, figuratively, of course. Putting those thoughts aside and coming back to the facts at hand, I told her he would make it through this perfect storm come hell or high water, he wasn't going anywhere! He was just as determined as we were. Bring it on, we're up for it.

Matt was still experiencing neck pain and a CT scan (Computer Tomography) was ordered. It was discovered that a tumour had eaten away at one of his cervical vertebrae and caused a fracture in his neck. The German treatment had shrunk and destroyed the tumour and removed the swelling thus leaving the fracture unsupported. Any wonder his neck had been so painful. The neurosurgeon suggested that a neck collar be worn, however Matt declined because of the instability in his legs, and it would be a trip risk as he couldn't look down. This was going to be another adjustment that he would need to take into consideration with his body.

In March 2016 after speaking with Kate and Richard we decided to see if we could import Ektomon. This drug had never been dispensed in Australia, and there would be many hoops to jump through to be able to do this. Firstly, we needed Martin to speak with Dr N at Hallwang. The clinic had never released this treatment outside of Germany and it would take a lot of convincing and paperwork to get the ball rolling. RCA provided a team of expert negotiators that stepped in to assist. We also needed the consent of Michael Boyer, the director at the Chris O'Brien Lifehouse Centre in Sydney, for this drug to be administered. The initial application was rejected on the grounds that it was not a researched treatment known or used in this type of cancer. Matt contacted Michael and politely explained his situation, what he had been through and what had worked. He also noted that on their website there was a statement that read, "We treat all types of cancer, specialising in those that are complex and rare." This ticked all the boxes and Michael agreed to allowing the drug to be administered by Martin through Lifehouse.

Next was the hurdle of the Therapeutic Goods Administration (TGA), which required an evidence-based letter which Martin scripted. RCA's team of experts were instrumental in getting this unique treatment into the country for Matt and they also funded the first treatment. This was a world first introducing gold standard cancer care into Australia. In June 2016 we had six doses of Ektomon arrive at Lifehouse. Unfortunately, we were unable to import the antigen treatment that the Hallwang clinic used, as this was still in a trial phase.

There were lengthy instructions of how to administer this treatment, and although it was administered slightly different here, we were extremely relieved that we did not have the financial burden of returning to Germany again. This was a huge win all around. Although completely worth it, the prohibitive cost of the flights, accommodation, treatment, and loss of income placed an enormous amount of pressure on our family unit. It also meant that Matt did not have to endure another lengthy trip, We could run both businesses and be earning an income, plus we would be at home with a lot of support around us. Most importantly, Matt could begin to get his life back on track again.

> *"I learned that courage was not the absence of fear, but the triumph over it. The brave man is not he who does not feel afraid, but he who conquers that fear."*
> **Nelson Mandela**

In August 2016 Matt was feeling and looking stronger. Unfortunately, his right leg that had suffered the nerve damage was still giving him problems as he endured the foot drop and the pain in the sciatic nerve, plus his left leg was still weak. He had been cautioned that his left femur was in danger of breaking as the cancer had been eating away the bone. He had also been told that if the leg did break it could prove fatal should the bone sever the femoral artery. This was a major concern for all of us, but another surgery at this point was also unadvisable.

Don't be Bitter be Better

Exciting escapades

Matt decided that he needed a holiday, and I could not have agreed more. He wanted to travel to Bali, and he asked if I would like to go with him. Bali would probably be the last place one would think of if their immune system was compromised, but he loved an adventure and indulging in different cultures. I needed a holiday as well, and I couldn't wait to board that plane, feel the warmth of the tropical sun on my skin and relax for a few days. Once again, my bag was three quarters full of matt's supplements and herbal formulas to keep him well and avoid the dreaded Bali belly.

Bali 2016

Bring It On!

I believe this trip was instrumental in putting the spark back in Matt's life, to be independent of the medical system, and open his world that had become shuttered for the last two years. This was another carrot, and soul food for Matt. We hired Ketut, a personal driver who took us off the beaten track, to explore villages, temples by the sea, restaurants by the beach and the rainforest at Ubud. We dined in the zoo's five-star rotunda restaurant with lions on the other side of the glass and ate dessert with the meercats. We hiked to Uluwatu Temple where a monkey jumped on my back and stole my glasses which had us both in hysterics, fortunately the glasses were returned after a little food bribery. We swam daily in the pool, had massages, enjoyed the Bali fish spa, and relaxed with cocktails of a night.

One morning I decided to go for a walk whilst Matt was resting, before Ketut was due to pick us up for another adventure. It was already hot and humid, as I headed outside of the hotel grounds. After walking for approximately an hour and thinking that I was on a circular path that would take me back to the hotel I realised that I had wandered off into the backblocks. The further away I got from the hotel the fewer people could speak English. I knew it would take me at least another hour or more to retrace my steps and find the hotel, and Ketut would be waiting for us. I had been given a few bum steers along the way by well-meaning locals, who probably did not understand my accent. A motorbike rider pulled up next to me and the man asked, what was I doing all the way out there. Thank goodness that at least he could speak English, I was relieved. I told him where I wanted to go, and he said it was a long way and pointed in the general direction. As he was going in that same direction, in a leap of faith I asked him if I could have a lift back to the hotel. So, I jumped on the back of the bike and off we went, with no helmet but he delivered me to the hotel safely. I arrived back just in time for our next tour to start.

Protein Smoothie

Use this to improve muscle strength and to avoid wasting.

- ½ Banana or substitute this out for ½ cup of fresh berries
- 1 tablespoon of natural Greek or coconut yoghurt
- 1 tablespoon of LSA (linseed, almond, sunflower seeds)
- ½ cup of baby spinach leaves
- 1 teaspoon of probiotic powder
- 8 raw almonds
- 1 x egg
- 2 teaspoons of a whole food powder (multivitamin/mineral + chlorella or spirulina)
- Pea protein powder can also be included, to quickly add bulk (muscle and weight)
- Add either 1 cup of coconut water, or unsweetened oat or almond milk. (avoid dairy)

This smoothie recipe is a wonderful alternative to people who have low appetite or are unable to consume solid foods and for those people who have lost weight due to treatment or illness. It quickly helps to rebuild the cells and improve overall wellbeing.

Chapter 10

Dogged Determination

Towards the end of 2016 Kate from RCA had approached Matt and asked if he would be willing to give an interview to a reporter from Channel 9's, A Current Affair (ACA) to highlight his medical situation. This would emphasise and bring awareness regarding rare cancers, the lack of support and the huge financial strain placed on the patient's family. We were the perfect candidates for this interview as this rare cancer had already cost us $785,000 in 18 months, and it was still early stages. The ACA team and Kate came to our house in December and interviewed Matt, David, and me. We were advised that the story would go to air in the week prior to Christmas. We were optimistic that it would be excellent exposure to raise funds for this wonderful charity. For one reason or another the interview was not aired until after Boxing Day, when the ratings were at their lowest and most people were away on holidays. This was a missed opportunity and an unfortunate outcome; we were very disappointed for Kate and Richard.

> *"The real winners in life are the people who look at every situation with an expectation that they can make it work or make it better."*
> **Barbara Pletcher**

Matt was slowly but gradually regaining strength and he was determined to re-establish his independence and to return to work as soon as possible. The company he worked for, the staff and his bosses had been incredibly supportive throughout this illness. Matt still had a myriad of physical challenges, but he had a dogged determination to be productive, purposeful and contribute once again. He loved the technical challenges of his job and decided to recommence work in May 2017. He had tried to do this several times before, but the disease had taken over and it became untenable. For him to recommence work it would mean moving to Newcastle, finding accommodation and being three hours away from us. David had driven Matt up to Newcastle prior to him starting work to speak with management, and they agreed he could re-commence work two days per week and then reassess if and when he felt ready.

Prior to recommencing work, Matt, Alex, and two friends, Joe and Dan, decided to fly to Japan to visit Mick as it had been eighteen months since their last catch-up. I was apprehensive about Matt going especially with the foreboding warning about his leg, but sometimes we just need to let go. The trip was not without its challenges, however sometimes events come along to test us. What happens on holidays stays on holidays, and all they said, with a smirk on their faces, was they had a fun time away. It was great that they all got to spend time with Mick, and it was nice for us too. Out of sight, out of mind, gave David and me the chance to be with each other and wind down. One of the boys had developed a cold whilst away and passed it on to Matt who presented with mild symptoms upon his return, but the associated cough seemed to linger for an unusual length of time.

Dogged Determination

Matt found a share terrace house in Newcastle East, which was the perfect location for him as the beach was a two-minute walk away, there was a supermarket around the corner and the harbour was nearby. The smell of the saltwater saturated the air, and I knew that this area would be good for Matt. The terrace had very steep stairs up to the bedrooms, and to have a shower it was necessary to step over a knee-high rim and into the bath. The poor design was dangerous, considering Matt's balance was not great, both legs were weak, and he did not have full strength in his left arm. One slip in the bath or on those stairs could have been disastrous. As we left him there to fend for himself one couldn't help but to be concerned. We commenced travelling to Newcastle regularly to check on his welfare and to see if he was coping and to provide a friendly face. Those first few months he struggled with his energy levels and fatigue as his body was unaccustomed to the extra workload.

The cough he had developed appeared to be more frequent and irregular for Matt who due to squad training had developed lungs of a long-distance swimmer. This turn of events raised questions at home concerning possible disease progression. It met the scenario, but we didn't want to alarm Matt. This was the elephant in the room we could sense, and no doubt Matt could feel, but no one wished to acknowledge its existence. He was due to see Martin and was due for another scan. The PET scan showed that he had now developed tumours in his lungs, which unfortunately explained the cough, and once again led us to question how much dogged determination needed to be summoned to knock this disease on its head. Martin recommended that Matt now go on low-dose chemotherapy tablets. We knew that chemotherapy had not agreed with him in the past, and this was not an intervention that we willingly supported.

After speaking with Kate from RCA, we managed to get an urgent appointment with Professor David Thomas who is head of the Garvin Institute at St Vincent's Hospital in Darlinghurst, Sydney. We discussed Matt's extensive medical history plus emphasised his extraordinary resilience and resolve, considering the determination of this tumour and everything that had been thrown at it. He explained that he would like to put him on the MoST program as part of a clinical trial. Molecular Screening and Therapeutics program (MoST) is an innovative approach bringing new treatment options for advanced and incurable cancers. New treatment options are targeted (or personalised) to the genes and proteins of the patient's cancer, instead of their cancer type. Matt's purse of treatment would be a two-part targeted and individualised immunotherapy course taken over twelve months. Matt quickly completed the paperwork and Professor Thomas promptly initiated the processing. Less than two weeks later after numerous blood tests, and scans Matt commenced the treatment program, which consisted of being closely monitored whilst undergoing IV infusions of the immunotherapy. Amazingly after the first treatment the persistent cough Matt had since May diminished. What an incredible result. He responded positively to the immunotherapy, and he was advised it would be available for as long as necessary. It would be an initial twelve-month program and review upon completion. His strength gradually increased enabling him to take on more days at work.

Prior to commencing the program, the tumour behind his left knee had increased in size as had the tumour mass growing in the quads in his left leg. The sarcoma surgeon requested a CT scan of Matt's hips and legs and then offered Matt a referral for a Psychiatric assessment if he didn't agree to having a femur and hip replacement on the left-hand side. This was melodramatic but emphasised the urgency and severity of his current condition. The femur only had about three-millimetre of bone left before it would break. So, the decision was made for that surgery to take place in March 2018.

I had booked a work trip to Sri Lanka with other naturopaths and herbalists to stay in an Ayurvedic Village and to visit a Ayurvedic Hospital, as well as a five-star integrative cancer treatment hospital. It was something I had been really looking forward too. Matt's surgery was to take place one week before I was due to leave. The surgeon understood Matt well and had successfully performed numerous surgeries on him, so we trusted him implicitly. He had previously told Matt that his tumours had not read the rule book on how to behave. After the surgery and during visiting we looked at Matt's legs and saw one was noticeably longer than the other. We thought it may have been the angle that he was lying in bed, perhaps one hip lower than the other. We asked him to straighten up, but it made no difference to the leg length. Once again, blind Freddy could have seen the error. When the surgeon arrived, Matt asked him about it. Upon examination he assured Matt that the ligaments and tendons needed to adjust, and it may take a day or two. Two days later the leg had not resized, and the surgeon realised he would have to re-operate. Another medical mishap. How many stuff ups can one person endure? Unbelievable!

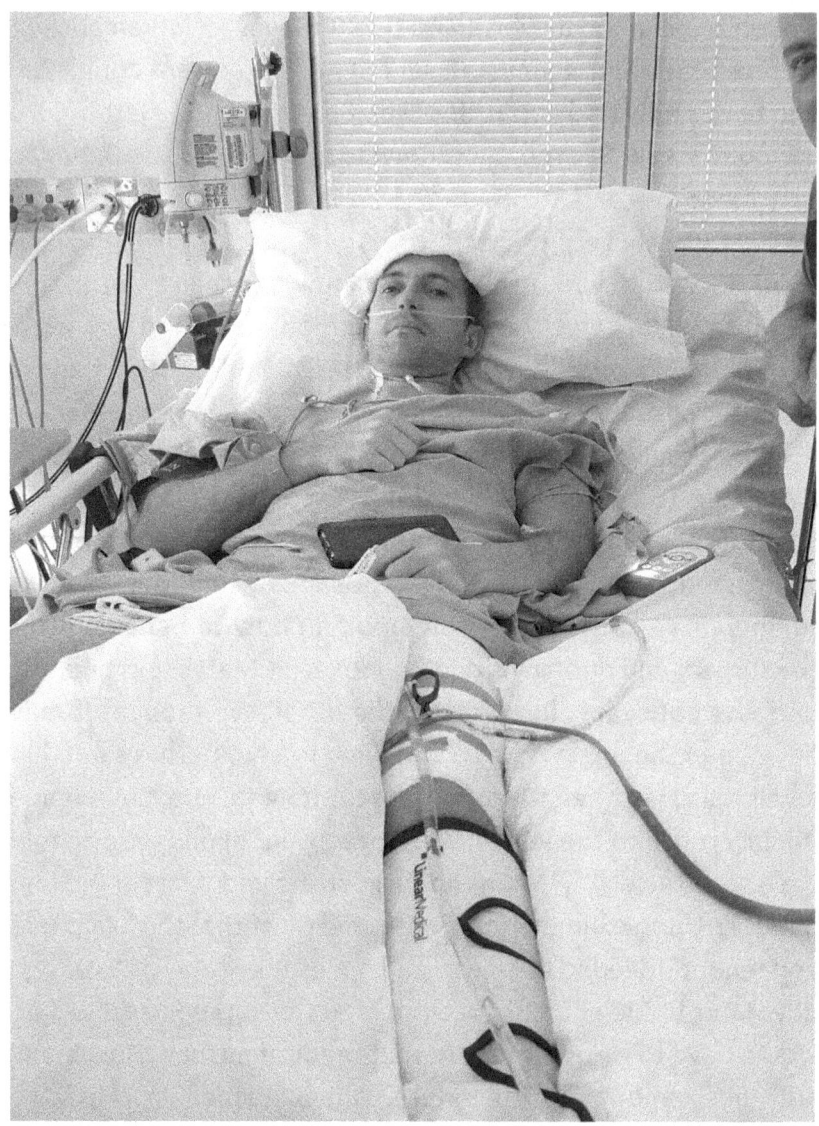

Matt leg surgery

I was concerned because this was another major surgery Matt was asked to undergo and it was leaving me little time to see him recovered, or to supervise and dispense the personalised remedies needed to speed his recovery. I was feeling very uncomfortable having to leave him in this predicament. I had hoped to be present for at least a week after surgery, now the second surgery was happening two days before I was due to leave. This time they got it right. Like the saying goes, "Measure twice, cut once."

"If you don't like something change it. If you can't change it, change your attitude."
Maya Angelou

Matt had a long road ahead of him of re-learning to walk, but he had set himself a target to be back at work within six weeks. I was still in two minds of whether to travel to Sri Lanka. I needed to go on this trip but was in a quandary and felt terrible leaving Matt who was still in hospital. I trusted David wholeheartedly with looking after everything including Matt's needs, plus Alex and Belle were there for backup. With less than twenty-four hours before flying out I made the decision to go and boarded the plane with no turning back. I just needed to focus on the week ahead.

Oxygen mask

After leaving the airport and travelling by minibus for five hours, we were nearing our jungle village destination when it became apparent that the phone reception was either patchy or non-existent. This was a blessing in disguise, as it gave me a chance to indulge my senses, relax, meditate, breathe, and let go. Our accommodation was mud huts, with dirt floors and no windows and doors and just days prior to our arrival three villagers had been killed by wild elephants. We could hear the elephants at the edge of the village of a night-time, and we were warned not to leave our huts after dark due to the danger. I loved listening to the noises in the jungle of a night, in particular hearing the apes and elephants calling to their mates. I encountered a snake in the open-air shower, giant spiders on the mossie net overhanging the beds, and monkeys watching our every move. This experience was great, it was back to basics, primitive and grounding. I was glad I had stepped out of my comfort zone and decided to come away on this trip. This back to nature jungle experience was my soul food, and it was just what I needed after all the chaos the family had endured.

The last few years had taken it's toll, and I noticed it once we hit the village. Undergoing some of those Ayurvedic treatments were very challenging, but it also gave me time to reflect and to heal. The large freshwater lake was a refreshing change to the heat, and it was peaceful to float in the middle with no one else around. I have been practicing yoga for over thirty years, but there was something incredible about doing yoga in the jungle on a rock with monkeys overhead. It was that deeper connection to nature, the self, breathing, and life. It was an awakening, and this was the sabbatical my body and mind had craved and desperately needed.

> *"What doesn't kill you makes you stronger."*
> **Friedrich Nietzsche**

Chapter 11

Rebirth From the Ruins

September 2018 marked thirteen months on the immunotherapy trial and the results were favourable. To start with, there were no new tumour sites plus there was no additional activity from existing sites. Each month that Matt was on the immunotherapy we could see a marked improvement in his energy, and his weight. He had weaned off the stronger pain medication he had been prescribed for the sciatic nerve stroke at the end of 2017. This was a huge adjustment for his body and his nervous system, but he persevered through sleepless nights and nerve pain to be rid of these addictive substances. Little by little, step-by-step we were seeing the old Matt emerge and it was exciting. His body was slowly starting to recover, and he was beginning to rebuild muscle. Coming off the immunotherapy finally meant he was unshackled from all the drugs he had been taking for the last four years. Freedom at last, normality was returning. His body could finally tolerate full-time work hours without feeling exhausted, and travel with his job was now back on the agenda. This was a win-win for Matt and his colleagues.

From the onset, I had made a promise to take Matt to Machu Picchu (golden carrot) when he was well enough. He still had this carrot in his sights, and he was working towards it. We would take that trip to Machu Picchu once he felt strong and able. His left leg was still giving him trouble, particularly as the skin had not entirely sealed after the second femur replacement. It was swollen and red at the surgery site, and once again he needed a surgical procedure to clean the wound. This procedure would be repeated twice more without success.

It was frustrating and we needed to think outside of the box, as the orthodox medicine was not working. It appeared that the tissue in the leg had been compromised by radiation and repeated surgeries. This is not an uncommon occurrence for patients requiring surgery after chemotherapy or radiation, and Matt was advised by the surgeon that it may never resolve. We sought a private wound care nurse to help clean and reduce inflammation of the wound, however, with all her knowledge and training, the opening persisted albeit cleaner. The wound can be an inconvenience especially when it starts leaking at inappropriate times, and needs the dressing changed, but Matt just takes it in his stride.

Matt was feeling well enough to finally take the plunge in to the dating scene after being single for the duration of this illness, which was now four years. Four years in your twenties was a long time to be out of the dating scene, however, his energy had needed to be placed into his own health and healing. Now, he was ready to focus his attention on finding a compatible partner. After searching for some time, he did find somebody, whom at first seemed genuine and trustworthy but this front soon unravelled, revealing her true nature. This was a major disappointment at the time, but reflection showed this break-up was a blessing in disguise.

Rebirth From the Ruins

"The purpose of our lives is to be happy."
Dalai Lama

Christmas 2018 was a jubilant occasion. Matt handed me a card in which he wrote he was feeling stronger and was now ready to tackle Machu Picchu. This was very exciting, uplifting and a truly joyous revelation. It was a major milestone, and he had finally reached it, and now we had a lot of planning ahead of us, and the excitement was building. We were unable to depart before September 2019, as David required major surgery to alleviate pain that he had been persevering with. He was booked to have a double knee replacement in January 2019, and it would take some time with rehab to achieve a reasonable level of mobility. This meant a backlog in my diary that took months to recover from and free up time away from clients.

David was in hospital for eighteen days, and once he was home it was a matter of juggling work commitments and ferrying him to and from exercise rehab. Unable to drive for six weeks, we were fortunate to have Alex and Belle ready to assist when required. I had hoped we would be done with hospitals for a while, but David had put up with excruciating bone on bone pain for the last three years and had been biding his time until Matt was stable and independent.

Planning the trip to South America and Machu Picchu was tantalising Matt's strengths. He meticulously organised our flights, our bus trips, visas and looked at intricate details that others may have overlooked. I booked the accommodation and the taxis to meet us at the airport. I had a list of major attractions I wanted to see, as did Matt. There was some duplication of places he had already been to, but this worked in our favour as he knew what the best attractions were. We were both so excited, as this had been on my bucket list for years, and for Matt the realisation that the carrot was finally coming to fruition. Mid-September 2019 we boarded the plane for South America and buckled ourselves in for the twelve-hour flight. As soon as we were in the air, Matt's competitive nature kicked in, as he dealt the playing cards ready to win. I knew then and there that he was psyched up and ready to conquer the Peruvian mountains. The majority of that twelve-hour flight was spent with Matt trying to smash me at cards, and him winning often.

> *"However long the night, the dawn will break."*
> **African Proverb (Plaatje)**

Flying into Cusco via La Paz the air was palpable with excitement and anticipation. The view of the mountains was stunning, and the carrot was getting closer by the minute. We had decided to stay at Ollantaytambo, a quaint little town full of ancient ruins, steeped in history. It had a central main square with cobblestone laneways leading off in various directions. We had booked a room in a guesthouse that overlooked a mountain with intricately carved stairs that accessed ruins and led onwards all the way to the summit. We had no sooner dropped our bags in the room when Matt looked out the window and said let's go. He was on a mission. I looked up at that mountain and the thousand steps to get to the top and I thought how on earth are we going to do this. I was worn out after getting up extremely early for the plane trip, then the long drive to this pretty, little ancient town.

I was a little concerned about Matt's balance and stability, especially with the unevenness of the cobblestones and the giant staircase that lay before us. I needn't have worried though, as he raced ahead of me to the top. The altitude and the stairs did not worry him at all. We spent the afternoon walking the trails around the mountain and investigating the ruins of this ancient city. As he stood at the top of the stairs and beheld the town below and the

Peruvian mountains surrounding us, his energy appeared as large as the mountains themselves. He looked amazing, and I could see this was really feeding his soul. This place was so spectacular and awe inspiring it was difficult to imagine that where we were headed the next day, would surpass this panorama.

At 6:40am the next day, we boarded the train to Aguas Calientes on our journey to Machu Picchu. As the train snaked its way over rivers, passed quaint farming villages, travelled through a rainforest, then along the fringe of enormous mountains our anticipation was reaching fever pitch. Aguas Calientes is the town located at the base of the mountain upon which Machu Picchu sits. From here we boarded the bus to take us up to the entrance gates of Machu Picchu where we recruited a private guide. As we stepped through those entrance gates it was like stepping into another world. Perhaps it was a metaphor of leaving all the things that no longer served us behind, and there was plenty to leave at that gate. The unrelenting stress, the illness, the draining and nearly life destroying treatments, strained relationships, financial burdens, and the physical incapacities due to the disease. Stepping through that gate onto sacred ground, was about embodying gratefulness that Matt had survived and not only survived but he was thriving.

The power of belief

From mid June 2014 until 2018 Matt endured 12 surgeries, 47 rounds of radiation, 13 sessions of chemotherapy, 30 Monoclonal antibody and 7 subcutaneous Antigen treatments (german), 4 rounds of double immunotherapy, 9 single immunotherapies plus

Don't be Bitter be Better

11 Hyperthermia treatments. A super human effort by anyones standards and now was strong enough to be here at Machu Picchu. We were stepping into freedom, personal growth, and manifesting great health, happiness, and stability. As far as spiritual experiences go this would have to top the list. Walking up the stairs to one of the highest points of Machu Picchu and staring down at the ruins surrounded by fog, added to the mystical aura of this ancient city. Standing at the edge of the mountain and viewing the scenery before him, Matt's chest was puffed up, he was standing tall, smiling, and looking very proud as he had finally reached the golden carrot. This was a rebirth from the ruins in more ways than one. He had reached the pinnacle and now it was time to start a new chapter.

The next day we travelled to the Sacred Valley, and to Cusco, a mini metropolis of ancient ruins, the poor, well-to-do, beautiful heritage buildings, and an attempt at modern architecture. We flew from there to La Paz in Bolivia where we investigated The Witches' Market on a town walking tour. We travelled to Lake Titicaca which the ancient Incan culture believe is the birthplace of the sun. We visited the Isle of the Sun and hiked up two hundred stairs at altitude to reach the fountain of youth. Matt sailed up those stairs without getting out of breath, however our two guides and myself struggled because of the altitude. It is said if you drink from this fountain that you will stay young forever. There were three spouts of water from a natural spring coming out of this fountain which represent heaven, earth, and hell. I was determined to put that water all over Matt. Whether the fable was fact or fiction I figured he needed all the help he could get. Most of these ruins have a narrative that comes from folklore that has been passed down or carved in stone. I feel many of these narratives have some level of truth to them, although I'm not sure about staying young forever.

Rebirth From the Ruins

Machu Picchu

Isle of the sun fountain of youth

Next stop was Argentina and on to Iguazu Falls. These waterfalls are breathtaking and awe-inspiring. Nature can put everything into perspective and just watching the power of the water going over those falls was mind blowing. We are just mere specs on the face of the earth fighting for survival. We jetted up the river, went underneath the falls and had an amazing time. This place was mesmerising, the sheer magnitude and force was awesome.

Next on the itinerary was Patagonia to visit the ice bar and to see Perito Moreno Glacier. This huge glacier with its mountains of white peaks, iridescent blue sheets, and deep crackling noises as it moved was breathtaking. You could have easily drowned in the extraordinary sensory overload of the crispness of colour, the coolness of the snow, and the enormity of the glacier. We had seen so many incredible aspects of nature and amazing things across five countries, and I feel so fortunate to have experienced this with Matt.

Coming up next was Santiago in Chile. The place where it all began, and I would soon see where Matt was living and where he was working. Santiago is a beautiful modern city boarded by the Andes Mountains. Matt's apartment was in a nice part of the city and not too far from his work. Whilst we were in Santiago, Matt attended work at the office for two days, leaving me time to explore. It was wonderful to meet his old boss and his co-workers and to see the rapport he had with them. They were very supportive of Matt when he had moved there in 2014, and when he needed to return home in a hurry. His boss had asked Matt if he would like to come and work for him again. South America is a traveller's paradise with its unparalleled beauty of the Peruvian Mountains, glacial lakes, Patagonia, salt flats and Iguazu Falls. This fateful trip was a huge sense of achievement especially for Matt, and for me to see where it all started. I felt he had come full circle, and this was closure.

> *"Healing is a matter of time, but it is sometimes also a matter of opportunity."*
> **Hippocrates**

Chapter 12

Hope Strength Resilience

Many have asked, how did you get through this turbulent time that life never prepared you for? Personally, I use the metaphor of having a newborn baby, as opposed to being handed a teenager. The newborn commences quietly, and gradually develops demanding more and more attention. As new parents you adjust your life and routine to accommodate this irreversible event. If you were handed a hormonal teenager, it would be a hell of a shock as you didn't get the opportunity to grow with it. This diagnosis began like the newborn as it didn't come with an instruction manual, behaved in ways that no one could comprehend and developed akin to a pubescent monster having total disregard to the consequence of its actions. Various forms of discipline were attempted with limited success, yet perseverance prevailed and gradually the monster was tamed, more so through…

Strength – to undertake the challenge

Resilience – to endure the adversity, and,

Hope – that the universe is backing you.

Don't be Bitter be Better

"One who gains strength by overcoming obstacles possesses the only strength which can overcome adversity."
Albert Schweitzer (1875-1965)

Looking back there is a group of attributes that have benefited us which I would like to share but please don't ask me their origin. Some say it's nature while others say it's nurture, personally I think it's more like playing cards and best using the cards that you have been dealt.

Having a positive mindset and a glass half full approach to life and the problems thrown at us played well into our hands, as did the ability to look at everything logically when emotions were running high. If a problem seemed insurmountable, we were able to break it down in to smaller, manageable projects and deal with them. We worked as a tight knit team to problem solve and support each other. Tenacity, focus, determination, and resilience are traits that would characterise my approach to life, and as they say, the apple doesn't fall far from the tree, with Matt mirroring these attributes. Some days we were exhausted, and we felt like we could have collapsed, but there was no time for being fatigued. It was a matter of digging deep every single day as we had a mission to accomplish, and we were determined to succeed. I would say we have strength and resilience in spades. Coming back to my metaphor I believe most mums develop a strength to get through all those nights of sleep deprivation, screaming babies, lack of privacy and exhaustion, and to come out the other side smiling.

"Cancer can be the scourge of human demise, but it can also be the impetus to let go of detrimental patterns and enact positive change." These are my own words that I have uttered to many cancer patients during consultation. Perhaps I think differently to many, as I do think outside the square, and navigating the disease progression certainly takes an 'outside the square' approach to work. Acknowledging that necessity is supposed to be the mother of invention, hence existing outside the square, was like stepping over the fence that carried the sign; do not proceed beyond this point. The answer was out there, and I regularly took leaps of faith to find the answer. My natural science background reminded me that matter could not be created nor destroyed, merely rearranged, and trust me, I was going to rearrange this hideous mass.

In the blink of an eye the body's immune system can miss the mutation of an otherwise healthy cell and the survival of the fittest protocol benefits this rogue misfit as it divides and replicates undetected securing a stranglehold around vital organs and vascular structures. Matt's health went from being fit and healthy, to knocking on death's door within seven months. He endured the best and the worst of the medical system and amazingly not one specialist, doctor or nurse in Australia ever considered equipping their patient with a healthy eating program. Nutrition is the cornerstone of good health and luckily, I went that extra yard and ensured that Matt was provided daily with a balanced diet full of fruit and vegetables. Cancer thrives on sugar as tumours consume up to thirty times more sugar than normal tissue. For PET imaging, patients are injected with a small amount of a radioactively marked sugar which, once in the body, reaches those organs and tissues that consume a lot of sugar.

I watched in horror as his hospital meals frequently were stacked with desserts or starchy bread, cakes, and biscuits. Undeniably, you are what you eat, and these hospital meals were setting an appalling precedent for what a patient should be consuming when they returned home. Without a doubt, this diet was going to make you into one giant raging tumour. Conversely, the specialist oncology clinic in Germany placed a great emphasis on whole foods, omitting processed goods and plating up appealing and nutritious meals that fed your body the essentials to support a healthy immune system while starving the unwelcome tumour. In every encounter I sought out the take home message of starving the tumour. A poetic justice that I adopted with delight.

I am a great believer in mind body medicine, and that one must treat the whole person and not just the disease. The core of my naturopathic training was acquiring the skill and knowledge to thoroughly and accurately undertake a differential diagnosis to list all possible conditions or diseases that could be causing the given symptoms. It is determined by reviewing patient history both emotional and physical, considering recent pathologies, undertaking an iridology examination, and developing a practitioners perspective connecting the symptoms to the source. In the instance of cancer all too frequently prolonged stress precedes a diagnosis. Bearing in mind that mankind has existed relatively unchanged biologically for at least a few thousand years, when our bodies primary source of protection was the fight/flight mechanism. Either way the cascade of stress hormones was short lived, what is termed acute in duration. Fast forward to the last two hundred years or so and witness the emergence of prolonged stress (chronic). The basic needs of life became more reliable, such as housing, drinking water, food, and heating but the emergence of unresolved dilemmas had arisen. Ongoing issues with finances, relationships, work/life balance to name a few all have a cumulative effect on the body's adrenals and ultimately the immune system's ability to cope. Any wonder that a few mutations may slip past the guard.

The best medicine is to resolve what is causing the stress and move on. In clinic I frequently encounter clients presenting with ongoing ailments that quick-fix pharmaceutical medications may mask for the course of the treatment but return, and occasionally more severe, after the tablets run out. Often the slippery slide into poor health begins with disrupted sleep followed by seeking out comfort foods and becoming lethargic with minimal exercise. All to often the billions of microorganisms that live in our gut are starved or drowned in alcohol, that is if they survived the inevitable course of antibiotics. Without a functional gut biome, nutrients are not absorbed, resulting in diminished cognition and a compromised immune system. In naturopathic medicine I take notice of an individual's constitution, which determines their body's resilience and the ability to tolerate neglect. Some people drink, smoke, and eat poor diets all their lives and live to be one-hundred years old. They are gifted with an amazingly strong constitution. For the rest of us that lifestyle is a recipe for disaster. So, when the chips are down, put down that bag of chips and go for the healthy options.

Yoga became my coping mechanism during these dark days. It provided me with the ability to seek peace and tranquillity with the added benefit of stretching and toning exercises all in the often-cramped quarters of a hotel room. Embedded in my yoga routine is the practice of mindfulness meditation which allowed me to step aside from the mental game of twister and bring my thoughts back to the here and now. Together, these techniques calmed and soothed both my body and brain. Even though I am an accredited Yoga teacher and well versed in putting together a class session, I find it convenient to sometimes opt for either a yoga class or an on-line session as it allows me to experience yoga as interpreted by other presenters. This provides the added benefit of being able to totally immerse in the experience without taxing the mind that I am trying to rest and re-energise. Those fortunate enough to have found yoga as their go to coping resource, understand the nature of Buddhist and Hindu teachings, that we are not a body, but we have a body, and we are not human beings having a spiritual experience, but we are spiritual beings having a human experience. We are more than a body.

> *"There is no separation between mind and body...*
> *Self and other co-arise and fall away all the time."*
> **Deepak Chopra**

Have goals to work towards. I have spoken about the 'golden carrot' throughout the book. Having goals to work towards, a purpose, or a reward allows for motivation, builds excitement, and increases happiness, which improves overall wellbeing. This completely changes the focus away from the disease to a pathway of invigorated purpose. I feel that it is important to take timeout regularly to nurture the soul, indulge the senses and avoid feeling enslaved to the daily grind. Find your Manyana and never underestimate "vis medicatrix naturae," the healing power of nature. I regularly partake in Shinrin-yoku (forest bathing) which has been recognised in Japanese culture for centuries. It means, taking in and utilising all of one's senses, in the forest atmosphere. Not simply a walk in the woods, it is the conscious and contemplative practice of being immersed in the sights, sounds and smells of the forest. It was designed to combat stress and death and we now know that inhaling the oxygen from the trees, the essential oils from the leaves, feeling the sunlight and wind on the skin is life extending and imperative to good health. Whether by good luck or careful consideration, the location of the German oncology clinic on the doorsteps of the famous Black Forest provided patients and their families the opportunity to experience the spiritual aura of forest immersion.

Out with the old. What isn't working for you is working against you. Often these behaviours arose during your formative years and have become the schemas by which you measure your actions and reactions.

Hope Strength Resilience

Just like a house, if the foundations are not solid it will warp and tilt, so too will your perception of reality. Time for a renovation. Removing substances, obstacles or behaviours that may be preventing a cure is paramount to gaining clarity in your thought process. Sometimes it is about letting go of people that may be creating negativity in your life. This is a good time to take stock and reassess what is important to you right now. Bear in mind the quote that is attributed to Albert Einstein; "The definition of insanity is doing the same thing over and over again and expecting a different result."

I know that I am not alone in hoping for my children to live happy, healthy, and rewarding lives, however sitting back and letting the universe take care of the future is simply wishful thinking. Matt may not have recovered if we hadn't applied every ounce of effort we could muster, plus some more we never knew we had until it hurt. We knew Matt was always hurting more and yet he never complained. Even on the darkest days we kept the focus on tangible alternatives, not allowing ourselves to resort to unreliable and untrustworthy too good to be true propositions, although any help was greatly appreciated. The situation was darn hard and real, and we needed to keep the response just as focused and real.

In my role as a Naturopathic Specialist, I can attest to the use of individualised, professionally prescribed Herbal Medicines to improve overall vitality and wellbeing and to aid in the recovery process. From the outset Matt was on a personalised prescription of herbal medicines and homeopathy that I would change frequently according to his constitution, emotions, energy, pathology results, surgery, and medications. This was part of his daily regime that he took religiously throughout the treatment phase. The importance of this holistic integrative approach was not only advocated by me but also corroborated by my peers and the doctors at the private oncology clinic in Germany. The proof was in the pudding or was that the Black Forest cake?

Strength is a word that we have heard often throughout these trying times in our lives. There's no question at all about Matt's mental strength and unwavering focus with all that he had to endure. His priority from day one was to beat this disease, to back himself and to step up to the challenge. His catch cry was 'go hard or go home.' Is strength innate or is it learnt? I think it's a bit of both, but ultimately one must believe in themselves and have strength in their convictions. The focus must be on being better and not bitter about the diagnosis, or what has happened to the physical body.

Matt is fortunate to be surrounded by family and friends. They came from far and wide to be by his side during lengthy stays in hospital or when he was at home recuperating. He had a core group of mates from primary school, work colleagues, university friends, doctors and nurses collectively wishing him well. This was a global community of friends some from Scotland, the UK, America, and Europe sending messages for a speedy recovery. The power of friendship cannot be underestimated. The support, the laughter, the kindness that surrounded Matt was profound and no doubt helped with the healing process.

The hope that I do convey, is that Matt's story as seen through the eyes of a mother and practitioner, inspires strength and resilience to tackle head-on whatever challenges that life throws at you and rise above being bitter, until you are better.

> *"You either get bitter or you get better... You always have way more choices than it feels in a moment of stress. The choices are yours."*
> **Josh Shipp**

Afterword

It is now eight years post the original diagnosis and I would like to finish this story on a positive note by saying that Matt is doing exceptionally well. His last immunotherapy, treatment was in September 2018; however, he still has regular check-ups with his medical team. It is all about keeping a healthy work, life, love balance. He has found his soulmate, an incredible, authentic, sensitive girl and they make a great partnership. He regularly swims in the ocean, bike-rides, enjoys long beach walks and he lives with some beautiful, caring but hilarious housemates. There is never a boring moment and there are plenty of card and board games to be had.

He loves his job which allows him to travel, and he is still with the same employer that recognised his potential and enticed him to work in South America. The company, the management and staff have been incredibly supportive and understanding. He has just completed the build on his own home and recently moved in. This is a dream that had been put on hold for five years that has now come to fruition. He remains in close contact with both work colleagues and friends from all around the globe.

Michael married Arisa in 2020 and they reside in Japan with their baby girl, Alex and Belle also married in 2020 and are the proud parent of a baby girl. Simon and Kayla and their children reside in Queensland, and David, Ella and I are still in the family home in

Engadine. We are as busy as ever running the clinic and bushwalking and swimming in our spare time.

How I feel

For four years, from 2014 until 2018, I felt like I had been placed in an old twin tub washing machine with one side gentle wash and the other side on the spin cycle. Everyday there was some new drama happening, and just as I thought we might be able to just soak and relax, the spin cycle would start. There was no time for relaxation as time was of the essence. Constant researching, working, juggling, being practitioner, mum, wife, daughter, and negotiator required a lot of persistence and energy.

There is no doubt that life throws us all lessons along the way, and we must deal with them. What we learn from them can come down to perception, expectation, belief, and outlook. One thing I know for sure is that every single lesson is an extremely personal experience and a journey into the self. Each person will have a different viewpoint and attitude to each challenge. All we can do is focus on the now, and how we manage and behave during these difficult times.

I consider myself fortunate that I work in the field of holistic health and mind, body equilibrium. The knowing and understanding of human behaviour and the body set the scene, for what could have been the ultimate annihilation of a fit, healthy young man. I am more than thankful every single day, that we got through this in one piece, and that Matt had the tenacity, and willpower to get through. I am also thankful that we were not 10 years older than

Afterword

we were at the time of diagnosis, as the energy required to get through this was enormous.

Here are some words of wisdom I would like to impart

> Don't roll over and give up, and do not be passive. This is not an option.
>
> Your life is worth fighting for, give it your best shot.
>
> You are so much stronger and resilient than you think. You never know until you are tested.
>
> Surround yourself with positive, supportive, reliable friends and family.
>
> It is okay to take a breath. Everyone needs time out sooner or later to recharge.
>
> If you know something is not right speak up. You must use your voice.
>
> Focus on the *now*. Don't dwell on what might have been or project into the future. All we know is now and that is where the energy should be placed.
>
> Don't second guess your maternal instincts. A mother knows her children best. After all they grew inside her for nine months.
>
> There is always an answer, it is a matter of finding it. Persistence pays off.

> Determination, tenacity, and dedication are required to get through most trials. Chin up!
>
> Hope! Instil hope for you and your person. Without hope there is nothing.
>
> Seek integrative care. It is a must for all cancer or chronically ill patients. It is the bridge between modern medical practice and traditional medicine and allows for a better long-term outcome for the patient.
>
> Use a qualified naturopath or herbalist for traditional medicine. Only seek advice from someone who is well studied and certified in the industry and understands pharmacology.
>
> Smile, you will come out the other side and the sun will shine again.

I would like to finish with the quote from Clare Boothe Luce, ***"There are no hopeless situations; there are only men who have grown hopeless about them."***

Matt's story has inspired many people, and by writing this book I hope that many more people will feel encouraged to pursue holistic solutions to their health problems, and seek integrative care. The best health is achieved by utilising the best of both worlds. A medical team that is willing to work alongside a professional, qualified and registered herbalist or naturopath. You can do this and achieve amazing results.

About the Author

Jennifer was raised in the suburb of Oyster Bay, a beautiful slice of country in Sydney's southern suburbs. Her childhood was spent discovering the unfenced and open surroundings, including swimming in the river and exploring the mangroves in her backyard. From a young age, she would pick, taste, and eat all sorts of plants, including the roots of weeds, and succulents, which may have been an innate knowing that led her down the current path of herbal medicine and naturopathy. Many days were spent with her best friend, Dee, climbing mulberry or loquat trees, gorging on oranges, peaches, nectarines, or anything else they could select from the garden.

Her parents Elva and Jim had a deep love of nature and thus the family home and large yard was filled with a menagerie of animals, abundant vegetable gardens and fruiting trees. Both parents instilled a sense of independence, responsibility, freedom of speech and respect for the environment. The weekends were spent either bushwalking, fishing, swimming, or exploring natural surroundings and this is something that she still enjoys today. Jennifer and her family all are avid travellers and embrace the experiential sensory explosion when encountering a new environment and culture.

From a young age Jennifer developed the courage to think and act independently when she created a school petition to remove a grumpy new primary school principal, and to have the old principal reinstated. This perhaps was the start of her courage and ability to negotiate and seek resolution for others as much for herself. She can evaluate a situation quickly and acts accordingly without apprehension which is testament throughout this book.

Her father Jim had wanted to be a doctor, but unfortunately his parents could not afford the University tuition fees. Her mother would take her to a herbalist when she was young to help treat her asthma. Having her father's inquiring mind and her mother's preference for natural remedies, plus her organic affinity for 'weeds' and health, led her to her current path. She met her soul mate and kindred spirit, David in late her teens and they married not long after. They are the proud parents of four boys and have four lovely grandchildren. When the children were young, and whilst running a demanding business with David, she commenced University studies in Health Science and Naturopathy. Additional studies included Nutrition, Herbal Medicine, Kinesiology, Iridology, Homeopathy, Cancer Supportive Care Medicine, and Yoga.

Jennifer has taught numerous courses over many years and has imparted her wisdom to upcoming students enthusiastic to learn. She is a regular speaker at cancer support groups, at hospitals, gyms, community groups and has been a guest speaker at an international conference. She is a keen advocate of mind and body medicine and Integrative care. She previously managed Her own Yoga, Pilates and Meditation studio for thirteen years, whilst concurrently running her integrative care clinic. Today both David and Jennifer along with Ella (the dog) reside in The Shire, working as practitioners in their well-known holistic clinic, Traditional Herbal Remedies. She remains passionate about the health of her clients and family and educating people on how to improve their overall wellbeing.

Don't *be* Bitter *be* Better

Jennifer Webster

Jennifer Webster is the Author of Don't be Bitter be Better, a true account of an aggressive cancer battle. She is the senior clinician at Traditional Herbal Remedies, a clinic located in Sydney's Southern Suburbs. She is a Master Herbalist, Naturopath, Nutritionist and Kinesiologist and is a passionate advocate of whole health education within the wider community.

For over 23 years Jennifer has successfully changed the lives of thousands of people who have sought her expertise in mind body medicine and integrative holistic care looking to reclaim their wellbeing as well as their health and vitality. She is a mother to 4 boys and a grandmother and intrinsically understands life's ups and downs and what it takes to get through.

Jennifer has a Bachelor of Health Science Degree/Natural Medicine, Advanced Diplomas Naturopathy, Herbal medicine, Nutritional Medicine, Kinesiology, Iridology, Homeopathy certification, specialised certification in supportive care medicine, International Yoga Instructor and Cert IV workplace training and assessing.

She has been a keynote speaker at an International conference for Herbalists and Naturopaths and she is a regular guest speaker at hospital support groups, charitable organisations and community groups. Jennifer has also been a regular health writer for a local newspaper, and has instructed a number of natural therapy courses over the years, helping fellow practitioners to upskill and educating community members to improve their body awareness and holistic health knowledge.

Speaking topics:

Matt's Story. From terminal to terrific.
You've been given that diagnosis now what?
How to master your mind
5 crucial elements for great health

Jennifer is available for

- ✓ Keynote speaking
- ✓ Retreats
- ✓ Half day sessions
- ✓ One on one sessions

www.traditionalherbs.com.au   TraditionalHerbalRemedies   traditionalherbs   Jen@traditionalherbal.com.au

Acknowledgments

When Matt was diagnosed, he was quickly surrounded by his family and friends. They came from far and wide to visit and to be by his side during his lengthy stays in hospital. They would arrive armed with their deck of cards and board games ready for a challenge. They would sit with him and watch the football or a movie or just sit and talk for hours. During his hospital stays he accumulated more friends. Some were doctors and nurses, and others were other patient's visitors. He was in constant contact with friends on his phone through messages, social media or email all wishing him well and a speedy recovery. The power of friendships with the collective get well message cannot be underestimated. The support, the laughter, the kindness that surrounded Matt was profound and in my view poetic. "You reap what you sow."

There were many people that either helped financially, physically, or emotionally during this time and without their generosity and kindness it would have made this experience even more challenging. We are incredibly grateful and thankful. Dee, my soul sister and most trusted ally, who was prepared to jump on the plane to Germany even though she has an intense fear of flying, who drew down on her mortgage to help get us there, and who spoke to me every day just to check-in, was a godsend and I cannot thank her enough. Then there are other amazing friends such as my neighbour Gail, Michelle and Alan, Steve, Leanne, Monique and Tim, Elizabeth,

Don't be Bitter be Better

Rosanna, Helene and Helen, all who have known our family for years and who went the extra mile to support us.

We would like to thank all our family for their support and caring thoughts that no doubt has helped Matt. Michael, Alex and Simon, their partners and families were there all the way. To Brian for his generous financial donation to aid with medication and my brother Rod, for his generous donation and for rallying the troops and generously handing me a financial lifeline if needed.

I would also like to acknowledge Matt's large medical team here in Australia, that went the extra mile, and the doctors and staff from Hallwang clinic in Germany. Matt's employers, who kept the communication lines open and for their amazing level of support. Kate and Richard Vines from Rare Cancers Australia. An amazing couple making a huge difference for anyone that is diagnosed with a Rare Cancer.

Last but not least is David. He has been my rock and soul mate for over forty years. He has been there through thick and thin, utilising his biological science background to research options to discuss with Matt and the medical team. He is intuitive and I feel that we can tackle any challenge together. Without him in our camp, I know we would have struggled much harder to achieve the outcome that we did.

"Many hands make light work."
John Heywood

Testimonials

I have been down the long cancer road more than a decade ago and one of the positive things to come out of it all was meeting Jenny. She is so supportive, empathetic, compassionate, and knowledgeable. She supports my physical, mental, emotional, and spiritual bodies through her amazing healing modalities and wisdom. I am incredibly grateful that our paths crossed as Jenny has assisted me to explore tools to live my best life.

Donna Johnstone

I have been a personal client of Jennifer Webster's for over ten years, but it was her talk when I was a facilitator with YWCA Encore that really shone the light on her knowledge. Jennifer's compassion and understanding with the ladies was fantastic. Our participants had nothing but praise for her knowledge and willingly answering their questions regarding their breast cancer diagnosis. With so much knowledge and understanding on cancer and how it effects people as a whole, both physically and mentally, Jennifer is nothing but excellent.

Di Albrecht - Retired Encore Facilitator

Life is but a journey and when the major challenges hit when you least expect them, your life is certainly turned upside down in a matter of seconds. Jennifer was introduced to me through a neighbour after I was diagnosed with breast cancer. They say the right person appears at the right time in your life when you really need them. Jennifer guided and supported me both physically and mentally when the going got tough. You certainly need someone from outside your own personal circle, someone you can share your inner thoughts with, how you are really feeling about what is happening to you. Jennifer was this person.

Fifteen years later, my health has improved dramatically as has my attitude towards life. The healthier you are, the happier you are, and with Jennifer's expertise I am looking forward to enjoying watching my grandchildren grow as well as experiencing the joys of living for myself and along the way returning to Jennifer's clinic for regular check-ups.

Petrina Warner - Retired

I have been seeing Jennifer regularly for many years now. I am very grateful for her support and understanding, along with honest input in my health and wellness. Whilst sometimes confronting, I can honestly say I am leading a much healthier and happier life thanks to both Jennifer and David from *Traditional Herbal Remedies*.

Kim Oxford - Accountant

I will be forever grateful for Jenny and her services, for her healing and life-giving self. Her guidance has helped me overcome and grow through some of the most challenging times of my life so far. I truly believe I am a better person and now a better mother having met her.

Tammi Toohey - Horticulturist

Testimonials

Nothing but sincere gratitude to Jennifer in helping me get back on my feet.

After a severe reaction to chemotherapy and a two-month hospital stay that left me weakened by massive pulmonary embolisms and very malnourished, I was unable to look after myself at all. Having never been ill in my seventy-two years, this was by far the greatest challenge I ever had to face. I had never been to a naturopath before, but I was desperate and Jennifer came very highly recommended to me.

After a week following Jennifer's individualised regime, I started to walk short distances unassisted. After a month I was able to board a plane and enjoy a holiday with my family, and after six weeks I moved back into my home and started looking after myself again. Three years later I am physically strong enough to do almost everything I had done before, such as my workouts at Curves, playing tennis, working in my garden, and spending time with my family.

Jennifer listened to me then and continues to listen to me today. She understands the pace her patients need to go at to feel comfortable, and most importantly she gives very clear guidance. In my case, following her recommendations allowed me to regain my independence, one of the greatest gifts of all. I cannot recommend Jennifer enough, particularly to those like me who have a cancer diagnosis but will not let it defeat them!

Madeline Lerch - Retired

Don't be Bitter be Better

Jennifer Webster is a highly regarded, vastly experienced and much sought-after holistic practitioner. Alongside her profession, Jennifer is a devoted wife and a loving and nurturing mother.

When one of her sons, Matt, was diagnosed with an extremely rare form of cancer at age twenty-four, Jennifer left no stone unturned in researching this formidable disease to treat her son. Through her dedication, many of the tumours have shrunk, some have disappeared, and no new tumours have been detected. It's amazing the strength many of us find when confronted with a dire situation. Strength that had no need to be called upon before, strength we didn't know we had. While many would succumb to fear and anxiety, from day one, Matt's will of iron, tenacity and positive attitude carried him through many surgeries, pain, and setbacks he has had to endure.

This story not only depicts the courage and unbreakable spirit of a young man dealing with a life-threatening illness but demonstrates the mountains that can be moved through a mother's love.

D. Williams - National Credit Manager

I first met Jennifer in 2017 when she spoke at the YWCA Encore program I attended while receiving treatment for breast cancer.

Upon conclusion of active treatment, I sought Jennifer's assistance to deal with the myriad of remaining symptoms and side effects.

Short of saying Jennifer performs miracles, I always find she actively listens to all my concerns and ailments (be they physical, spiritual, or emotional) and prescribes such wondrous gems that by the time I have my next consultation, I have all but forgotten that I had such troubles.

Jennifer is highly recommended.

Kylie Lynch (patient 2017-2022)

Notes

www.ingramcontent.com/pod-product-compliance
Lightning Source LLC
Chambersburg PA
CBHW050506120526
44588CB00044B/1391